# LEFT BEHIND

*A Mother's Grief*

# LEFT BEHIND

*A Mother's Grief*

Carol Kifer

PAZ PUBLICATIONS
*St. Olaf, Iowa*

*LEFT BEHIND:*
*A Mother's Grief*



Requests for information should be directed to:
PAZ Publications
P.O. Box 16
St. Olaf, IA 52072

Library of Congress Catalog Card Number: 98-91755

ISBN 0-9666014-0-8

First Edition, January 1999

Cover Design by Mike Meyer

PRINTED IN THE UNITED STATES OF AMERICA

*This book is dedicated to*
*Jeff Darrell Kifer*

*and*

*In memory of*
*Krista Lin Kifer*

# CONTENTS

# CONTENTS

## *ACKNOWLEDGMENTS*

*For their help in making this book a reality, I wish to thank:*

*My husband, Darrell, for his continued love and support--physically, financially, and emotionally.*

*My son, Jeff, for his willingness to share his feelings and philosophy of life with me and my readers.*

*My mother, for her consistent, unconditional, nurturing love and friendship.*

*My younger sister, Sher, who was only a phone call away when I needed someone to listen, to share ideas, or to encourage me.*

*Allison Kalscheur, for the rose used in the cover art.*

*Friends strong enough to endure the bad times with me. I won't mention them by name since they are humble, gentle persons, embarrassed by praise.*

*Strangers who comforted me with compassion and understanding, becoming friends as we shared stories of our past and dreams of our future.*

*My writer friends, for their encouragement, constructive criticism and publishing expertise.*

*God, for his presence in my life today, the gift of Jesus Christ, and the hope of eternal life.*

# PREFACE

What do you do when the one thing you said you couldn't live with has happened? How do you go on living when your child is dead?

This book was written to provide support for others who are searching for a way to survive every parent's worst nightmare--the death of a child. It began as a journal three weeks after the death of my fifteen-year-old daughter as I struggled to find an answer to these two questions. For a time, searching for answers became the focal point of my life, a life that had been totally redefined by the absence of Krista, my first child.

If you are the friend of a grieving parent, I hope this book will help you understand the depth of our grief. The death of a child is an event that we never get over. It is a reality we learn to live with. The healing is never complete. The wound is always there, a permanent scar, intermittently bleeding as it is reopened by special dates, memories, or triggered responses. When you understand our pain, you can help us.

If you are the unfortunate parent, I hope this book will make you feel less alone. Will you allow yourself to feel the pain of your own loss? Do you want to be happy again even though it seems impossible right now? Grieving is difficult work, but it need not be a solitary journey. There are many of us searching for direction in a life forever changed by death. It is okay if this book makes you cry--our tears will be our bond.

My story may be very different from yours, yet you will be able to identify with much of it. We are connected, you and I. Our children have died. We are part of a special club that none of us ever wanted to join. The price of admission is much too high.

Anger, despair, isolation, guilt, regret, intense physical and psychological pain--all these feelings are inevitable and necessary components of dealing with such an overwhelming loss. As I recorded my own feelings, I tried desperately to find granules of hope to cling to amid the painful task of surviving in a world in which I no longer cared to live--a world without my child.

Time may help, but time itself does not heal. People heal. I was fortunate in having a number of caring people come into my life at the right moments to aid my healing. It was the power of God working through other people that allowed me to survive the first year.

On the anniversary of Krista's death my tears flowed freely as I was forced to admit the reality that she and I were forever separated in this world. I had lived for a whole year without her. During the early months of my grief I hadn't believed survival was possible.

The good news is that we can live with the sadness. There is hope.

I know how a child's death hurts because I've been there; I'll always be there, because my daughter will never come home to me again in this world. I've been left behind.

*Carol Kifer*
*Monona, Iowa*
*1998*

# PART I

# DEATH

*(Author's Note: Although this section of the book appears first, it was actually written last. Only after working through my grief during the first year and a half following Krista's death was I finally able to allow myself to relive and record the events of the days immediately after she died. I recalled fragmented portions of the events occuring in that time span, noting the details as my memory moved in and out of focus. Purposely devoid of emotion, these chapters depict the initial state of shock which allowed us to function. Our existence seemed to be a constant stream of motion.)*

*Time is irrelevant now.*
*I don't know what day it is.*
        *I don't care.*

*There are only two days in my life--*
        *the last day Krista was with us,*
        *and today, when she is gone.*

# THE TRAGEDY

When I arrived home from work Friday night at 5:00, I found a note from our daughter lying on the desk: "Mom, Gone to Jamie's to stay overnight. Any questions, just call. Love, ♥ Krista." Leaving notes for each other signed with a love heart was standard procedure at our house.

I called Jamie's number and chatted with Krista a few minutes. It had been a rough day for her. That morning she had broken up with her boyfriend of over a year. A fifteen-year-old girl needs her friends at a time like that. She was looking forward to spending an evening out with the girls.

We were having unusual weather for December in Iowa. Although there was about a foot of snow on the ground, the temperature was unseasonably warm. Fog had been a consistent concern for about three weeks.

As I looked out the kitchen window, I noticed the lights of a car coming up our dead end road. When the dog did not bark, I knew it was Darrell coming home from work, and busied myself with dinner preparations.

My husband and I were just finishing supper when Krista stopped back home briefly around six o'clock. She needed to get her activity ticket, which granted free admission to school events, and her $15.00 allowance. The girls were going to a basketball game at the high school. Following Krista to the door, I made my usual worried comment, this time about how foggy it was. A quick hug and a knowing smile were promptly delivered by my daughter as she sought to console me.

"Don't worry, Mom. It'll be all right. We're just going to the game. See you tomorrow."

Darrell and I talked a few minutes about whether we should have let her go out on such a foggy night. We both agreed that she needed her friends to cheer her up. It was only two miles to town, and the girlfriend she was staying with lived right in Monona. It would be all right.

Our eleven-year-old son, Jeff, was also staying overnight at a friend's house and going to the same game. I didn't worry as much when he was out because I knew an adult would be driving, not an inexperienced teenager.

The two of us spent a quiet evening at home and went to bed after the ten o'clock news. Within minutes my husband fell asleep beside me, exhausted from a long day at work. The last sound I heard before drifting off to sleep was the whistle of a train in the distance.

A loud, crashing sound awakened me. What the...? I envisioned a gigantic stack of large, heavy boxes toppling someplace in the house.

"Darrell, did you hear that? Someone must be in the house!"

All was silent. Darrell woke and said he had heard nothing. How could he not have heard? I glanced at the digital clock showing 11:25 P.M. and thought of Krista. Something was wrong! Where was she? Oh yes, she was staying overnight at Jamie's. Why did I have such an uneasy feeling? I thought about calling Jamie's house to talk to Krista just to put my mind at ease, but I knew how embarrassed she'd feel. Instead, I prowled around the house a little, checking out the basement and the upstairs to see if I could locate the source of the crashing noise, but I found nothing out of place. Perhaps I had been dreaming, but it seemed so real. Returning to bed, I said a little prayer to God to quiet my fears, asking him to watch over Krista, and I was able to relax again, believing He was with her. I stayed awake until midnight, assuming she would be safely in for the night by then.

## *THE TRAGEDY*

The banging on the door awoke us. I glanced at the digital clock--3:20 A.M.--Saturday morning. Oh, my God...it's Krista. Leaping up from the bed, I looked out the window and saw the police car.

"Darrell, get up! Someone is at the door! It's Krista! I know something has happened to Krista!"

We went to the door together. I saw two police officers in uniform. Our minister, wearing a black derby hat and looking very solemn, stood beside them. It reminded me of a scene from a horror movie. Was my worst night-mare coming true? If only I could wake up and discover it was not real, but the sick feeling in my stomach murmured, it's real.

A former conversation with my daughter invaded my mind. I had confided to her my worst fear--that some night the police would show up at my door to tell me she had been killed in a car accident. At the time she'd called me overprotective and told me not to worry so much. My greatest fear was coming true....

I don't remember opening the door to let them in. I know I was reluctant to step toward the door, afraid they were going to say something I didn't want to hear.

"No, please, not my Krista..." I pleaded, as the three entered.

There had been a terrible accident. The car had hit a train in the fog and burst into flames. All three teenagers had died instantly of head trauma.

"Do we need to go someplace, to identify the body?"

We were told that it would not be necessary to view the remains to make an identification. The bodies had been burned beyond recognition.

"Was she wearing any jewelry?" one of the police officers asked. "The other two people were identified by their jewelry."

"No." She wasn't wearing any jewelry. Her class ring had just come that day. She hadn't even seen the ring yet. Maybe the officers were mistaken. Maybe Krista had not been in the car?

The police had investigated to be certain Krista was involved before coming to tell us. Only minutes before the accident, she had been seen in the car with the other two students.

Darrell was silent.

"What do we do?" I asked.

"You need to call the relatives."

"Tomorrow?"

"You need to call them now."

"I can't."

"It will be on the news in the morning." The officer handed us a card with a phone number on it. "Call this number after you've notified the relatives. Is there someone we could call? To be with you?"

"No. We're fine."

"How about Langhuses, Jim and Linette?" our minister suggested.

"They'll be asleep."

"I think someone should be here with you. What's their number?"

Darrell accompanied the officer to the kitchen to use the phone.

I wanted my mother to know first. I needed my mother to put her arms around me and make it better. Could she do that? I couldn't tell Mom. Instead, I decided to call my brother, Dennis, who lived in the same Wisconsin town, thinking he could go over and tell her in person.

No answer. I left a message on Denny's answering machine for him to call me right away. (Later he told me that he had called back the next morning, and that I told him about the accident. I had no recollection of that conversation.)

I realized I had to call Mom myself. She answered on the sixth ring.

"Mom?" I could barely talk.

"Carol. What's wrong?"

"Is Jerry there?"

"Yes."

"I need to talk to him right away."

Pause. "Just a minute."

*Jerry is the man my mother loves. I love him, too, because of his devotion to her, and because he is a caring, compassionate person.*

"Hi, Carol."

"Jerry." My voice was shaking, crying. "There's been a car accident. Krista is dead." I couldn't believe what I was saying.

"We'll be there as soon as we can, honey."

"You have to tell Mom, Jerry. I couldn't."

"I know. I'm sorry." He paused. "We'll be there in a couple hours."

I made two more calls, one to my sister in Wisconsin and one to my dad in Florida. I have no recollection of the conversations, but my sister remembered her call clearly. Awakened from a sound sleep by the ringing, Sherri answered on the bedside phone.

"Hello," her sleepy voice whispered.

"Krista?" I said, disoriented.

"No. This is Sher."

She heard me crying on the other end. "Is that you, Carol? What's wrong?"

"She's dead. Krista's dead."

"Oh, my God! No! What should I do? Should we come right now?"

"Mom is coming."

"What happened?"

"An accident. The car hit a train. I always worried that she'd die in a car accident. I don't know what we're going to do."

"Do you want us to come now?"

"I don't know. Call back tomorrow." It was Saturday morning, but in my mind it was still Friday night. Time ceased to exist for us when we learned Krista was dead.

Darrell called his parents. By 5:00 A.M., the necessary calls had been made.

We went to pick up our son Jeff at his friend's house. Our friend Jim drove the van and the pastor rode along. We crossed the railroad tracks twice on our way there. Darrell and I sat together silently in the back seat. My thoughts were of the preceding night, as I tried to understand what had gone wrong.

*I trusted God to take care of Krista. Where was He? Maybe if I had taken action instead of ignoring my fears she would still be alive. Mothers are supposed to protect their children. I should have called Jamie's house! I should have done something!*

Jeff was still visibly sleepy as we led him out of the warm house into the waiting van, but the concern on his face was evidence he knew something bad was happening. Seated between Darrell and I in the back seat, he looked up expectantly, searching our faces for a clue to the reason for his interrupted slumber. I can't remember which one of us told him about his sister's accident, only the wetness of a little boy's tears as he buried his head in his hands. Our parental arms surrounded him in a smothering embrace, unable to let go of our remaining child. Jeff cried himself to sleep, eventually, in our bed, saying he just wanted to go to sleep and find out it was a bad dream when he woke up. We all wanted that....

The note! Where was the note? I retrieved the crumpled note from the wastebasket. The hastily scrawled note was suddenly precious, my last love letter from my daughter. *Don't leave me, Krista. I ♥ you, too.*

*PLEASE, GOD, let it be a terrible mistake.*

# THE FUNERAL PROCEEDINGS

When Jeff awoke Saturday morning, he discovered that a number of our best friends had already arrived. I think he knew the answer to his question before he asked it.

"Mom, where's Krista?"

"I'm sorry, Jeff." We sat in the bedroom with the door closed. I reviewed the story he'd heard earlier about the car accident.

"Maybe it's not her. Remember? The body?"

"She would have come home, honey."

"Maybe she's someplace else. It might be a mistake."

"I don't think so, Jeff. Her friends saw her in the car. She would have come home by now."

"I don't think it was her, Mom." He went upstairs to Krista's bedroom, the only one of the four upstairs bedrooms occupied since we moved into the house other than his own. He spent the entire day there, listening to CDs and reading *Teen* magazines, occasionally interrupted by the young visitors who whisked up the stairs to join him.

News of the tragedy spread quickly. Jim and Linette, who had come about 4:30 in the morning in response to the officer's call, remained with us the entire day, running the house, doing the chores. Mom and Jerry were the first of the family members to arrive. Other faces appeared throughout the day--friends, acquaintances, a few strangers.

The aroma of roast beef emanating from the crock-pot tantalized the stream of visitors. The refrigerator became filled with fruit salads and casseroles. Women from the church arrived with brownies and chicken soup.

Business people supplied pop, paper cups, napkins, plates. I was immediately grateful for their caring.

I don't remember the words that were spoken, only the faces of those who came. We shared hugs. We shared tears. Their continuing presence gave us strength to get through the difficult days ahead.

Midmorning we received a call from the funeral director. "What time can you come in to make arrangements?"

Silence. I didn't want to make arrangements.

"Would one o'clock be all right?"

*All right? Nothing was all right. My daughter was dead.*

"Okay, we'll be there."

---

We are sitting in soft chairs in a brightly lit room, discussing issues of relative unimportance. It's a small group--Darrell and I, Darrell's mother, my mother, and Jerry. We had asked Jeff if he wanted to come along, and we had received an emphatic "No."

A competent woman gently asks us necessary questions and jots down our parroted responses. She will take care of the details. She is aware of our fragile state, familiar with death.

Our minister is with us. He explains about the customary church funeral service. I say I have written something about Krista that I would like read at the service, but he is not interested in seeing it. He points out that we must focus on God's message of comfort at the service, not the person who died. *But my daughter is dead,* my mind shouts silently. When the minister asks us to choose two hymns for the church service, I immediately choose "Jesus Loves Me." This is not acceptable. It is not a good funeral hymn, he explains.

I am angry, but I do not show it because it requires too much energy. I look at Darrell. His face is red and he is straightening up, sitting tall in his chair. He is very angry, ready to explode. I do not have the energy for a confrontation with the minister.

"This isn't the time or place," I whisper to Krista's father.

*Darrell controlled his anger because of my request, but I made a big mistake. I should have allowed the anger, mine and Darrell's. It was justified. We are the parents. The minister was only a man doing his job as he interpreted it. The anger not released remains.*

Darrell selects "Children of the Heavenly Father" and "How Great Thou Art." Acceptable hymns, he has chosen wisely.

*Why am I doing this?* I ask myself. This isn't the event I want to plan for my daughter. I want to plan her Sweet Sixteen party, her graduation celebration, her wedding. I want to visit colleges with her, to shop with her for her wedding dress, to spoil the grandchildren she would surely give us. I want to plan her future, not her funeral.

We listen to the minister as he tells us how the funeral will be conducted. When he gets to the part about the burial, I cannot remain silent.

"Darrell and I decided we don't want a regular funeral service. We want to have the burial first, then a memorial service."

The minister explains that it works best to have a funeral service first and finish with the burial. That's the way it's done at St. Paul Lutheran Church.

This is not a debatable issue with me.

"I've been at other Lutheran churches where they do it differently. I can't end with putting my little girl into the ground."

Darrell agrees with me. He voices his concern that perhaps we will need to find someplace other than our church to have the memorial service. Perceiving that our minds are not to be swayed, our minister agrees to let us have our way on this point.

Why is everyone getting out of their chairs? Are we going someplace? Have we finished planning the funeral? I wonder what they decided. Does it really matter? Krista isn't here. That's what matters.

We walk down the hall to another room. It appears to be an auto showroom lined with a dozen shiny models featuring the latest styles. But instead of cars, caskets of various colors lined with fabrics of smooth silk and crushed velvet are on display. Why are we in this room? *Krista isn't here* is the message flashing in my robot brain. *Not here. Not here.* Everyone is looking at me. *Why? Why are you all staring at me? Am I supposed to be picking out the perfect casket? Is this my motherly duty? Not here. Not here.* I walk once around the room, looking for a clue. *Not here. Not here.* I cannot breathe. *I must get out of this place.* I point to one in the middle.

"She liked pink. That one, with the pink lining." *Not here. Not here.*

In one corner of the room are sample vaults. We must choose one to hold the coffin for the burial.

"You choose," I tell Darrell. *Not here. Not here.* I cannot leave the room fast enough.

Our stiff bodies return to the room with the soft chairs. We look at pictures in a book and select flowers for our daughter's farewell party. I want to cry, but I don't have the strength. *Please hurry. I can't stay here any longer.*

---

We were instructed to select the items to be placed in the casket with Krista and bring them to the funeral home by eight P.M.

"Do you do that when there isn't a body to view?" I asked.

"Sure. Bring whatever you want. Have it here by eight so we can seal the casket tonight."

At last I had a mission, something to do, something that mattered.

It became a family project. Darrell and I selected her prom dress first, recalling her youthful excitement on that special evening. She had written a beautiful story about her prom experience which she called "The Perfect Day." Tearfully, I wrapped the rhinestone earrings and necklace she had worn to the prom in white tissue paper. Her father added a photo of Krista and her date. We consciously avoided eye contact as we placed the mementos in a small box which I labelled, "Souvenirs of Your Perfect Day." We could not succomb to our emotions. We had things to do.

Jeff selected a stuffed dog he had given Krista as a Christmas present. The three of us and two of her best friends wrote letters to Krista because some things can't be left unsaid, even when there was no time to say goodbye.

The selected items were placed in a large plastic bag and delivered to the funeral home. It was much later than the scheduled time of eight o'clock, but the funeral director displayed neither anger nor surprise at our tardiness. He seemed to understand that survivors in the early stages of grief have no timetable.

Darrell and I didn't think we would be able to endure the hours of visitation scheduled at the funeral home for people to offer us words of comfort. Both our minister and the funeral director assured us the visitation was necessary, not only for the family, but also for Krista's friends and classmates. I wasn't sure they were right. My husband had confided to me an experience from his childhood, fainting in a funeral home. I wondered whether we would be able to stand the pressure. Neither Darrell nor I wanted to participate in this ritual, but we were coerced into it. We opted for shorter visitation hours than those suggested by our funeral director. On this particular day our emotions had to be locked up. We could not allow them to escape. We needed to stay in control.

*I will always be grateful to the knowledgeable professionals who insisted we participate in a visitation. They were correct. It was necessary, although we couldn't see our need for it clearly at the time.*

Because there was no body to view, we decided to set up tables with pictures and collections of objects representing special moments in Krista's life. We spent most of the day and evening selecting items for the display. There were huge photo albums depicting family times we shared during her fifteen years with us--birthdays, holidays, and that special vacation we had shared in Colorado the summer before--our last vacation together.

I stared at the picture of Krista sitting in the snow on the mountaintop, smiling proudly. She had made it to the top with her eyes wide open, overcoming her fear of heights. I never thought much about angels before, but sitting with the picture album in my lap, I wondered: Could it have been the touch of an angel that allowed us financial means to fly a family of four to Denver that June for only $20.00 so Krista could experience the exhilaration of looking down through fluffy clouds from atop the Rocky Mountains? It had been a special moment she shared with her Dad, as Jeff and I had remained in the car at that stop. That picture did not belong in the display. Her hair was not perfect. She always wanted it just right for photos. That picture was too personal.

Darrell and I had been "bumped" by the airlines on a business trip in Las Vegas only eight months prior. We had received a $1,000 travel voucher for free airline tickets. We could not have afforded our mini dream vacation without such luck. Was God's hand at work here granting us special memories to cherish in preparation for Krista's death? I had no answers, only questions.

I reached for a smaller album engraved with the words, "This is the Day The Lord Hath Made." It was my confirmation gift to Krista. It included a picture of her in her confirmation dress, wearing the gold cross she had purchased with her own money. Confirmation Day had been very special for Krista. It was the biggest celebration held in her honor during her too-short lifetime. At the beginning of the book I had typed this message: "If you want to be happy: Accept yourself as the special person you are. God created you. Greet every day as a special gift from God, an opportunity to experience life in its fullest. Try something new. Don't be afraid. Look for the joy in simple things--a sunny day, a walk in the woods, a hug from someone who loves you."

Krista's essays on "The Perfect Day" and "Best Friends" revealed a talent undeveloped. We filled one table with these essays and remembrances of school days and friends, a major focus of any teenager's life.

I decided to include a piece of reflective writing I had composed the morning after her death--the one deemed inappropriate for the memorial service:

*REMEMBERING KRISTA*

*God gave us a beautiful girl on loan*
*for fifteen years,*
*Now he has called her home*
*and holds her in his loving arms.*

*She grew into a wonderful young woman*
*with a special talent*
*for listening, caring and*
*making us laugh.*

*She was a teenager.*
*She loved pizza, movies, cruising,*
*"hanging out" with friends,*
*rock songs, Mountain Dew, and*
*chocolate.*

*She loved her pets.*

*We called her daughter, sister,*
*granddaughter, niece, Godchild,*
*cousin and friend.*
*We were her family,*
*and she loved us most of all.*

*We will miss her forever, and we thank you,*
*Lord, for the memories*
*that will keep her alive*
*in our hearts.*

Sunday came. The last of our relatives to arrive, only minutes before we left for the funeral home, was my father. He had begun the long drive from Florida a couple of hours after receiving news of Krista's death.

There was already a long line of people at the funeral home when we arrived since visitation for one of the other accident victims, Krista's friend, Jamie, was also being held there. That viewing had begun several hours earlier.

When I saw all the beautiful flowers surrounding Krista's casket, a flood of love poured over me. The exquisite, quiet beauty of these bouquets acknowledged a life that mattered. We had requested donations to a local children's home in lieu of flowers, feeling the money could be better spent to help children who were still alive. But I had been blind to the ability of flowers to speak so eloquently of love at such an emotional time. Those who sent them understood grief better than I. Never again will I request "no flowers" for one of my loved ones. I will send flowers more often.

Krista's grandparents, aunts, uncles, and cousins sat in rows of chairs in the middle of the room, strangers to the people arriving to comfort us. Two of Krista's best friends sat beside Jeff in the front row.

---

I am standing with my husband next to our daughter's coffin in the flower-filled room. Friends and strangers are offering condolences. I go through the motions of conversation, shaking hands, exchanging hugs, but I am not really here. I cannot feel my body. Is my body dead, too? I have no hands, no arms, no legs to hold me up. Only my face is here, smiling, carrying on. What is holding up my face?

I recognize the woman enfolding what appears to be my hand firmly in both of her hands. There are tears in her eyes. We had attended church together for many years in a town twenty miles away. The prayer chain. Suddenly, I know. They are praying for me, for our family. Who are they? They are all praying--fellow church members, friends, family, even strangers. I can feel their prayers. Are we being held up mysteriously in answer to their prayers?

---

We remained at the funeral home for five hours. There was a steady stream of people. I was afraid no one would come. The faces of those who took the time to come are etched forever on my heart--eyes filled with compassion, cheeks stained with tears, trembling mouths whispering words of sympathy. *Thank you for the hugs I needed so badly.*

I particularly remember the teenagers who came. They had lost three classmates, and this was a difficult time for all of them. Coming there was a courageous act. In addition to the sadness on the faces of Krista's closest friends, I noticed fear. Death was not a natural part of life for teenagers. Did they think their youth was a safety net? They were afraid, perhaps wondering who among them might be next to die an untimely death. I wished I could reassure them. But all I could do was return a few hugs, relishing the feel of a teenager's arms again, secretly imagining my daughter in each young girl's embrace.

When it was time to go home, I realized we had completely forgotten about Jeff. Where was he? My brother had noticed Jeff turning very pale, and had taken him out to get some air. The relatives decided it was time for him to leave, so friends had taken him to their home, where we could pick him up after the wake. The pressure was too great for a little boy whose parents didn't know he was there. Because of a TV camera waiting outside the funeral home, it had been necessary for a coat to be held over Jeff's head as he left.

*Thank you for taking care of our other child. We are overcome by our grief. We do not know what we are doing. We cannot think. We cannot feel. We are only going through the motions, doing what has to be done. Forgive us for doing everything wrong.*

As I tucked Jeff into bed that night on a fold-out couch we had moved into our bedroom, he asked, "Why did God give me a sister if I wasn't going to get to keep her?"

"I don't know, Jeff. Maybe so you'd have someone to play with when you were little. Maybe so you wouldn't always be an only child like your Dad. I don't know."

"It's not fair."

"No. It's not fair."

I was awake all night. My husband was exhausted and slept soundly beside me, snoring. But my mind would not be still. I finally got up and prowled the house, wandering aimlessly from one room to another, wishing for the privacy to wail and scream as I felt the need to do. Since our relatives had traveled so far to be with us, it was necessary for a number of them to stay overnight at our home during the days prior to the funeral.

I sat on the blue-flowered loveseat in the living room looking at photo albums, trying to cry silently as everyone else slept. Then Darrell's strong arms were around me, holding me, as I wept uncontrollably.

"Please, Darrell. Don't be strong for me. Cry with me."

"I love her so much," he whispered as the tears began to flow. We clung to each other desperately as we cried together. We were no longer Krista's mother and Krista's father. We became at that moment Krista's grieving parents, in it together. I was thankful to have married this special man who was strong enough to cry.

A difficult day lay ahead. I hated the thought of putting my little girl into the cold ground. She and I had talked of death, and what bothered her most was the idea of being all alone in the cold, dark ground. I remember assuring her the soul left the body immediately and dead bodies put into the ground had no feelings. I would need to remember that myself.

The morning of the funeral we visited the families of Derek and Jamie, the other two teenagers killed in the accident, in their homes. No words were necessary. We shared a common sadness. We were all preparing to bury our children. Darrell and I did not attend the other funerals--one was enough.

When it was time to leave for the burial, Jeff did not want to go with us, but I felt it was necessary. He was still acting as though Krista would be coming home again, and I thought witnessing the burial would be important to him later as he dealt with his grief. I told him to remember Krista was already with God in heaven, that it was just the body she no longer needed being put in the grave. I was proud of Jeff that day. Like the rest of us, he did what had to be done. Darrell and I needed Jeff beside us.

Many of Krista's classmates came to the burial. Some of them put flowers on her coffin after we left. We were the first to leave as soon as the committal words were spoken. I wanted to hide in the van with my husband's arms around me and pray that this day would end. I couldn't bear to stay at the cemetery any longer. Following the graveside committal service, we returned to church for a memorial service.

As we waited in the chapel, we received a letter from our previous pastor who had traveled twenty miles from Elkader to assist with the service. We had been members of his church for ten years before moving to Monona. The letter began,

*Dear Darrell, Carol and Jeff,*

*There are those who will say that Krista has died. I would rather say that she is soaring with the angels. Yes, your loving, beautiful, faithful daughter has been stolen away by that ageless enemy Death--yet there is a God who is loving her even in this moment.*

*This is the God who gave her life--the God who entered her life with love and faith through the Spirit at Baptism. And this is the God who has now mercifully received her into His loving arms in eternity.*

*Death is a powerful enemy--even among God's people. And when death takes a young person, even God's people discover a sadness that words fail to describe; an anger that is righteous and terrible. It's not supposed to happen this way. God's plan was (and is) for life.*

*The best way to go on is to live in the faith and confidence that all of God's promises are true. The best way to go on is to remember only the best. The best way to go on is to forgive everything.*

*We will never forget Krista's beauty and grace..."*

The letter ended "Your Friends in tears", and was signed by Pastor Jim and his family. That letter personalized the service for us. It was no longer just a generic, by-the-book formality. Pastor Jim was going to be there, too. He understood our loss--our sadness and our anger. His words reminded us that our daughter was safe in God's arms. After sharing the letter with other members of our family, I tucked it into my coat pocket as we walked down the aisle to the memorial service.

I remember very little about the memorial service other than the sound of two voices in perfect harmony as they sang "Children of the Heavenly Father," and the strong grip of my husband firmly holding my hand in his.

Krista's class sat as a group on one side of the church. Three years earlier she sat with the same group for the funeral of another classmate, a twelve-year-old boy who had died suddenly in a tractor accident. He had not been a close personal friend, but Krista had cried for several hours after learning of his death, horrified by the unfairness of it all. I remember her remarking that he had so many friends, he was so popular, he had so much to live for. She told me she knew if she died, hardly anyone would come. Krista was quiet and sensitive, and did not possess the outgoing personality required of those in the popular crowd. Remembering that earlier conversation, I was thankful for her classmates' presence at the service.

The women of the church had prepared a bountiful meal. I don't remember eating. I remember the faces of those serving us.

Three days had passed since we learned of Krista's death. The funeral was over, but our journey of grief was just beginning.

# THE AFTERMATH

The day after the funeral our relatives went home, where they would grieve in their own way. Many of their friends and co-workers would not be aware of their loss. They would not be surrounded by people who knew Krista. All of us were left without the support we had shared during the days following Krista's death.

The busy time was over. Others would get back to normal, but there could be no return to normal in our house. Our daughter was gone. Jeff's sister would not be coming home again. How could we possibly go on living without her? Now the real grieving started.

I read a newspaper account of the accident. I had assumed Krista had been dead only a short time before the police arrived at our home, that she had died early Saturday morning. But according to the *Cedar Rapids Gazette*, "The MFL/Mar-Mac students were headed to Postville for a dance around 11:30 p.m. when their car struck a train obscured by the fog....A 1983 Oldsmobile driven by Steva struck the 68th of a 91 car train. The three young people were killed instantly." Krista had died Friday night, not Saturday morning!

*I believe in extra sensory perception, particularly between a mother and her children. I've experienced it.*

When Jeff was two years old, he almost drowned in my parents' swimming pool. I was inside helping Mom with supper, peeling potatoes, when I had a feeling Jeff needed me. I ran outside, potato-peeler in hand.

"Jeff, where's Jeff?" I yelled at the men who were supposed to be watching him.

"He was here a minute ago."

Instinctively, I ran to the pool, saw him under water in the shallow 3-foot end, jumped in, and lifted him out. He was choking and coughing as water spilled from his mouth. How did I know that he was in danger?

*I know now the loud crash that awakened me the night Krista died was not imagined, but was the sound of the car slamming into the train. I sensed her danger. When I felt God's presence surrounding her, I had been able to go back to sleep, believing she was safe; but I hadn't realized at the time she was saying goodbye.*

Two days after the funeral, as I sat on the bed crying, my son put his arms around me and gave it to me straight: "Mom, I wish you wouldn't cry so much. It makes me sad when you cry. Krista wouldn't want you to cry."

Why was he concerned with what Krista would want? Did he still think she was coming back? I tried to explain to Jeff that I couldn't help it, that it hurt too much to have her gone.

My little boy wanted so desperately to make me feel better. "Mom, you've still got me. I heard on the radio about a minister who had all six kids die in a car accident. It could be worse."

Was he really only eleven? Had he overheard someone discussing this incident in relation to our loss? Was this wisdom on his part, or just a childish plea for his mother to notice he was still here? *I'm sorry, Jeff.*

"You're right, honey. We're still a family--you and Dad and me. I love you."

He looked relieved. Maybe it would be okay. Maybe Mom would stop crying.

I still had Jeff. And I still had my husband. Thank God, there was something left despite my overwhelming grief. Maybe if I could just get some rest...

When I called for an appointment to get some sleeping pills, the doctor agreed to see me the same afternoon. It had been four days since I last slept and I was physically exhausted. I knew it was important that I get some rest if I was going to be able to cope at all. I still had a family, a smaller family, but one that needed me to be well to take care of them. The sleeping pills worked. My mind rested, and for the first time since our daughter's death, I slept.

# PART II

# SURVIVAL

*(Author's Note: The chapters in this section are not in chronological order. Grief is a time of confused searching, not an orderly progression. Each chapter focuses on a single grief issue which may have spanned several time periods in my grieving process.)*

*LEFT BEHIND*

*I am trapped*
*in a complex maze of grief--*
*confusion, depression, rage.*

*The path to recovery uncertain,*
*I struggle to escape*
*death's suffocating grip.*

# PHYSICAL PAIN

I was totally unprepared for the physical pain that accompanied our grief. The heaviness in my chest caused constant pain in the weeks and months immediately following Krista's death. Sometimes I wondered if I was having a heart attack, although at the time I really wouldn't have cared. Deep physical breathing, sighing, seemed to become an involuntary reflex. Severe headaches plagued me as I concentrated on the mind-boggling fact that Krista was dead, yet I could think of nothing else. I was so physically exhausted that every movement was forced.

My husband experienced similar symptoms. He insisted upon carrying on business as usual at work, which helped him cope emotionally, but I was seriously worried about his health because he was so exhausted physically. When he wasn't working, he slept most of the time.

One night about two weeks after the accident, some of Krista's friends came to visit us. Visiting was difficult. It required energy that we did not possess. While we were standing at the door, saying goodbye to our visitors, Darrell suddenly collapsed. We managed to get him to the sofa in the sitting room, and I called the ambulance, in spite of his insistance that it was unnecessary. I didn't want to take a chance of losing him, too. When the paramedics arrived fifteen minutes later, they checked his vital signs and decided that he was all right and had just fainted from exhaustion.

The first month I had difficulty sleeping without sleeping pills. The muscles in my back, arms and neck ached constantly, as the stress tended to cause flare-ups of previous physical injuries.

I wasn't hungry. I ate when food was put in front of me, but the food had no taste. In spite of the calories consumed, I lost sixteen pounds in two weeks. I felt weak. It was as though all the nourishment that should have come from my food was burned up by all-consuming grief. I had no energy.

The stress showed in the condition of my hair and the added wrinkles appearing on my skin. The bags that formed under my eyes aged me. I wondered who this woman was when I looked at myself in the mirror. I looked old. I felt old. If I went to work during the day, I could do nothing more than lie on the couch at night and rest so I could get through the next day.

For my son, the physical manifestation of grief seemed to be a deep restlessness. He was energy in motion, unable to sit still for even a moment, needing to be constantly on the go. He ate continually. Jeff was exhausted by bedtime. His sleep was deep, with heavy breathing and snoring.

For the first six weeks Jeff complained of stomach aches every night at bedtime. Was he experiencing some kind of separation anxiety? We used to hear Krista and Jeff upstairs, laughing and talking when they were supposed to be sleeping. I guessed he was homesick for Krista. He missed their special time together.

It no longer surprises me when I read of an older couple who have been married for many years dying within a few weeks or months of each other. Perhaps they died from the pain of a broken heart that could not mend. Maybe the body cannot always overcome the physical effects of grief. Does the will to live die, rendering the body incapable of healing?

I remember wondering if it would always hurt this deeply, and being afraid that it would. But the worst of my physical symptoms subsided after the first four months.

# BEYOND PHYSICAL PAIN

Imagine the wonderful human thinking mechanism--the brain--as a well-equipped computer designed to control the human body and manage all functions through its master control panel. Suppose a malfunction in the control panel caused the computer to lock up so only one program would run. The result would be chaos. This is how I experienced the first six months of my life without Krista. My brain locked on the fact that Krista died, relaying the program over and over in my mind and allowing no other programs to run.

I was in a constant state of confusion. I would go upstairs to get something and forget why I was there. This might happen five or six times in a row. Sometimes I had to write down on a piece of paper what I intended to do so I could carry it out. I felt so absent-minded that I wondered if I was really losing my mind. Concentration was not possible. I couldn't play cards because I would stare at the cards and not know what I was looking for. The rules of the game temporarily escaped me. The only activities I could successfully participate in were watching TV, because it required no thinking on my part, and reading books on grief, because it fit into the program presently playing in my mind. I tried a number of diversionary activities--going to movies, school activities, an occasional social outing--but I found I was usually there only physically, while mentally I was still in my own little world. That world was very narrow, and the barriers were slow to come down.

I was obsessed with thoughts of Krista. I spent my time compiling scrapbooks with pictures of her and our special times together. I wrote poetry about her death and the implications it had on my life. Our love connection remained strong, and I searched for ways to hold on to her in her absence. This preoccupation made concentration on anything else very difficult.

I did not care whether I lived or not. I wished we had died together so I wouldn't need to feel the pain. I remember telling someone it would have been better if we'd accidently driven off the mountain on our Colorado vacation, so our family could have all died together.

I was worried about Jeff. He had quit talking about Krista a week after she died. One night after we had sent him into our bedroom to sleep, I noticed him sitting on the bed, hugging the teddy bear that his classmates had given him when Krista died. I sat beside him on the bed.

"Jeff, do you want to talk about it?"

"No."

"If you want to cry, it's okay."

Silence.

"Sometimes just talking makes us feel better. Do you want to tell me what you're thinking about?"

"No."

"I love you, Jeff. I really need a hug."

We held each other silently for perhaps five minutes. I cried, but Jeff didn't.

"Mom, if something happens to you and Dad, I won't have nobody. I'd be all alone." He took a long, deep breath. "I guess I'd have to kill myself."

Hearing these words from my eleven-year-old scared the hell out of me. "Jeff, I wouldn't want you to ever do that. "

"Think about it, Mom. If your Mom and Dad died, and your brother and sister, and me and Dad, your whole family, wouldn't you want to die?"

*Yes, I would*, I thought to myself. But to Jeff, I replied, "You'll never be alone, Jeff. Dad and I will probably live a long time, until you have a wife and kids of your own. But, if something *did* happen to us, you'd still have lots of people who love you--your Aunt Jackie and Uncle Denny, your cousins, Aunt Sher, Uncle Dave, your grandmas and grandpas.

"But you and Dad could die."

A dilemma--should I lie to comfort him or tell the truth? His sister had just died; he wouldn't buy the lie. "Yes, we could. But it's not very likely that we will soon. We'll probably be around to see your red-headed kids. You've got lots of friends, Jeff. You're a lovable guy. You'll always have people that love you."

The look of concentration on his face convinced me that he was thinking this over thoroughly. Of course he'd be worried about his future--one-fourth of his family was gone. Poor kid, so young to have so many worries.

"Jeff, Denny and Jackie told us a long time ago that if anything happened to us, you and Krista could live with them. They already love you. You'd have a bigger family than you do now. We made sure right after you were born that there would be someone to take care of you if ever we couldn't."

This seemed to satisfy him. He looked relieved as he crawled under the covers, ready for sleep. *Please God, take care of Jeff.*

Jealousy reared its ugly head at this time. I was jealous of those who still had complete lives. I tried reminding myself there are some people who want children who are never able to realize that dream, even for a short while. It didn't help.

Routine things that were once important to me no longer mattered. I quit participating in choir, womens' groups, and teaching Sunday School. I became an inactive member of the community organizations I had joined. Even my home didn't interest me.

It had been a weekly Saturday ritual for Krista, Jeff and I to clean the house together. We all lived there, so I felt cleaning should be a family project. Darrell worked on Saturdays, so we had excused him from this routine. Cleaning seemed so irrelevant now. Months passed before I even bothered vacuuming. And I didn't ask Jeff to help anymore. Laundry piled up. When Darrell or Jeff complained they were out of clothes, I'd wash a load of whatever they needed. My underlying thought was this: If we die tomorrow, what difference will it make if the house is clean, the laundry is neatly folded in the proper drawers, or the sparkling clean dishes are strategically arranged on freshly papered shelves? All the things I had lovingly done in my home as part of caring for my family seemed meaningless. Krista had died anyway.

Periods of depression following a death are very common, and may be heightened by special dates. It was so difficult to forget the lasting relationship I envisioned with my daughter when Krista was born and to live in the present.

It is acceptable to go to a doctor for help with physical ailments. But where could I turn for help with my emotional pain? There were no quick fixes, no magical pills. Professional therapy was very expensive and time-consuming, and I considered it a last resort. I embarked on an uncharted personal journey of grief. I had no map to follow, no timetable with which to graph my progress. I relied on perseverance, hope, my perception of God, and the loving kindness of other people to assist me on my journey.

*I miss having Krista with me physically. The emotional scars left by a loved one's death are invisible to normal people living normal lives; but those who have been there themselves look at the grieving heart with understanding and see the reality behind the determined smile.*

I participated in everyday life, however half-heartedly. I continued to work at my secretarial job, attended school functions, and went out socially now and then. Eventually, my malfunctioning computer began running new programs for a few minutes or hours each day. I had a glimmer of hope that there might be something left of life.

In the beginning a deep sadness surrounded everything I did. The joy of new experiences was overshadowed by the absence of the daughter who should have shared them with me.

Two years after Krista's death the sadness still lingers. I am again capable of experiencing joy, but I doubt very much that the sadness will ever go away. Some days it is still overwhelming. When I have a particularly bad day and nothing can bring me out of my depression, I give in to the tears, reassuring myself that today is only one day and I can live with sadness this one day. Tomorrow will come. I try not to think much about the future. Taking life one day at a time is my prescription for survival.

# GUILT

My screams awakened my husband and son four consecutive nights. I knew I was having a bad dream, but I could never remember it when I awoke. Finally, one night, as I was tossing and turning, Darrell woke me before the actual out-loud screams, and I was able to remember my dream.

Krista was running through a dark tunnel, being chased by a large faceless free-form monster; she was searching for me, yelling for help, expecting me to save her. I couldn't see the monster in my dream, only its huge shadow about to overtake her. I always woke up just at the point where the shadow was descending upon her.

I know nothing about dream interpretation; I believe the monster in my dream was "death" and I was having the dream repeatedly because I felt guilty about not being able to protect my daughter from death. I had allowed Krista to go out in the fog the night of the accident. I also felt guilty about having been relieved to learn she had broken up with her boyfriend that day. After discussing this dream with my husband and admitting my feelings of guilt, the nightmares stopped.

I had been an overprotective mother, always concerned for my children's safety. I tried to anticipate dangers and avoid situations where either of them could be injured. As a small child, Krista accepted my limitations, even when they were extreme. As she grew, she needed the freedom to explore, to take reasonable risks in life. It was difficult for me to let her go.

Krista led a short life, but a full one. Yes, my greatest fear was realized--she did die in a car accident. But even if I had never allowed her to leave the house, she could have died of a heart attack, cancer, aneurysm, or a host of other unknowns. I have come to realize that no matter how much we love our children, we cannot protect them from everything.

Regardless of how a child dies, parents probably experience some guilt feelings. We may feel we had a part in causing the death or just regret some of our past decisions in raising our child. We all wish we could be perfect parents, but the truth is that none of us can be. It is easy to look back and see our errors, but it is also fruitless. We made our decisions with the best of intentions using the information we had at the time.

We need to honestly face any guilt feelings, whether the guilt is real or imagined, and eventually find forgiveness. In some cases, this may require counseling. God always forgives. Sometimes, it is harder to forgive ourselves. Guilt is an issue that cannot be ignored.

# INTIMACY

From the time we learned of Krista's death until the day after the funeral, we had a house full of company. None of our relatives lived close, so it was necessary to provide overnight sleeping accommodations for many of them. Out of necessity, Jeff slept on a fold-out couch in our bedroom. However, that living arrangement continued for three months after Krista's death.

Sex was not an issue during the first eight weeks after Krista's death. Darrell and I were each too physically and emotionally exhausted to be interested. However, the need for closeness was very strong, not just between us, but also with Jeff.

We live in a large house. Our master bedroom is downstairs. Jeff and Krista had occupied two of the four upstairs bedrooms. Eleven years old at the time of his sister's death, Jeff wanted the security of being in the same room with us. We didn't object because we found it equally comforting to have him with us.

It was difficult having so little privacy. Darrell and I usually cuddled until Jeff fell asleep and then we'd talk in whispers. Bedtime was the most painful part of the day for us. During the early part of the day we could pretend Krista was just out with friends or in school. But since our family members were in the habit of giving each other goodnight hugs and kisses, it was impossible to deny her death when she wasn't here to say goodnight. I remember trying not to cry so I wouldn't wake Jeff, but the tears that dampened my husband's shoulder were beyond my control.

We began to feel the need for sexual intimacy, to renew our closeness as life partners, sharing everything, to feel completely connected again to someone in this world. A girlfriend of mine, who had been in a similar situation when her teenage son died, made it possible for us to have some evenings alone by allowing Jeff to stay overnight with her son. I was relieved to learn that her son had also slept in his parents' room for several months after his brother's death. The two boys were both only children now and they had become good friends.

I had some emotional problems engaging in sex after Krista died. Often in the middle of our love-making I'd start crying, unable to continue because it reminded me of the way Krista's life began, our act of love. I know Darrell was hurt by this reaction. In spite of the fact that Darrell and I had previously had good communication, I didn't discuss with him the reason for my tears. I felt the sex act was disrespectful to Krista's memory. I expected him to intuitively understand my feelings. But our needs were different. He needed the physical closeness, and I didn't understand. This was an issue that required a great deal of patience to resolve. Poor communication compounded the problem.

We encouraged Jeff to let us know when he was ready to move back upstairs, assuring him that he could remain in our bedroom as long as he wished. When Jeff wanted a room of his own again, we moved into another bedroom upstairs so we were all on the same floor. This made the transition easier. We remained upstairs for about two months, at which time Jeff suggested we move downstairs so that he would be able to stay up later without keeping his parents awake. He needed his privacy, too.

# KRISTA'S ROOM

One of the immediate problems for us was what to do with Krista's things. I was torn between wanting to give some of her belongings to other people to remember her by and wanting to keep everything because it had belonged to her.

One of the biggest mistakes I made was starting to give away her things too quickly. The day of the funeral I gave Krista's jewelry box to a cousin so she would have a remembrance of her. My son was very upset. One of the items in the jewelry box was a birthstone necklace Jeff had given his sister for her birthday, and he didn't want anyone else to have it. I gave another cousin a CD of the rock group Meatloaf that Jeff had given Krista for a Christmas present. I am appalled now at how insensitive I was to my son's feelings at the time. My only excuse is that I was in shock and not thinking clearly. I should have asked his permission before giving away any of her belongings. When he confronted me with his anger, I apologized and made a phone call explaining my mistake, so the items could be returned to Jeff. In the beginning I believe he still thought Krista was coming back, and he wanted to protect his sister's things so they would be there for her.

During the first few days after we learned of Krista's death, Jeff spent all his time in her room, playing their favorite CDs--Boys II Men, Ace of Base, Salt-N-Pepa, Bryan Adams. He lay on her bed reading her *Teen* magazines, the regular features she used to read aloud to him. The section in which readers wrote about their most embarrassing moments had been a frequent source of shared laughter.

Then, one day, Jeff's feelings about the room changed. He closed the door to her room and didn't go there anymore. I think it was the day he decided she was not coming back.

It is difficult to grieve as a family because each person is at a different point in grieving at any particular time. What may be helpful to one family member may actually increase the grief of another. This was our problem with "the room."

Our son was reticent about sharing his feelings with us. Jeff seldom volunteered emotional information unless we asked him specific questions. About six weeks after her death, however, he did come to me and ask if we would do something with Krista's room. My immediate reaction was to tell him that we weren't ready to do anything with the room. He was extremely angry and he yelled: "Just forget it. You and Dad make all the decisions around here. It doesn't matter how I feel. Do what you want."

I realized then we needed to listen. Jeff was reaching out to us for help, and as his parents, we needed to be there for him. Darrell and I had each other to share our parental grief, but he had no other sibling to share his grief.

I asked Jeff to explain to me what he thought we needed to do with the room. He said having the room the same made him feel like Krista wasn't really dead; it gave him hope that she was coming home again. He didn't want to keep thinking like that if it wasn't going to happen. He was right. Her room gave us all false hope, which we, as her parents, clung to desperately.

One of the reasons it is so hard for parents to alter their dead child's room is because doing so is an acknowledgement of the fact the child will not be coming home again. Every night when I got home from work I would go upstairs to Krista's room and look at her things, straighten them up a little, touch them. The three-foot Minnie Mouse she had purchased with her vacation money at Disney World was still sitting on the neatly made bed. When I hugged Minnie tightly with my eyes closed, she felt so soft, but the stuffed mouse clad in festive Christmas green and red, was lifeless. I kept expecting Krista to be there, but she never was.

I liked keeping Krista's room the same because I could fool myself into thinking she was coming home again. I was still waiting for her to come home. I wasn't ready to face the reality of a world without her. Not wanting to accept the permanence of her death, I secretly denied the horrible truth.

I discussed Jeff's request regarding the room with my husband. Darrell wanted the room left as it was. Because he worked long hours, he felt that he needed more time to spend in the room before we did anything with it. But I was worried about Jeff. Our son needed us to do something with the room to show him he was as important to us as our dead daughter--that his feelings did matter. After careful consideration, we reached a compromise. We needed to do what was best for our surviving child. We would move Krista's things into a different room and repaint her old room.

Before making any changes in Krista's room, we borrowed a camcorder and videotaped her room as it was so we could see it again whenever we needed to. This idea came to me from a friend whose child had died a couple of years earlier. The suggestion was helpful and practical. When the room of a child is described in detail, it is possible to glimpse that child's innermost personality. Their rooms encompass not only their belongings, but also past accomplishments and future dreams.

Jeff was not interested in helping with the room; instead, he went to one of his friend's homes on Saturday while Darrell and I worked on Krista's room. It was an all-day project, and I'm thankful we were able to do it together.

Krista had redecorated her room the summer after her thirteenth birthday. Together we had stripped the wallpaper, painted the walls pastel pink, and selected ruffled pink priscilla curtains and a matching bedspread. Her room was her private hideaway.

On one shelf of the bright pink bookshelf in the corner stood a collection of ceramic dogs and horses, her sixth grade obsessions. Stuffed animals crowded together on the second shelf. Another displayed six unusual music boxes, a collection she began in seventh grade after her grandparents had given her a musical clown figurine of Emmett Kelly, Jr.. Her favorite music box was an eight-inch porcelain doll with long, blonde curls, dressed in a festive green Christmas dress trimmed with red ruffles. When properly wound, the doll danced gracefully in a circular pattern to the music of "Joy to the World." The latest additions on the top shelf were two bowling trophies. The Sunday before her accident she had been thrilled by bowling her highest scores ever, 130 and 145. Athletics were not her strength, and she averaged about 100. There was one group of books on the bottom shelf, *The Babysitters Club* series, leftovers from her bookworm phase in fifth grade.

The wall above her stereo displayed posters of good looking guys. We used to call them "hunks"; now they call them "babes." Her favorite was a picture of a man in tight jeans, holding a bouquet of red roses behind his back, which read "Buns 'N Roses". She'd bought it when Guns 'N Roses was the latest rock group craze.

On her dresser in a tiny gift box were the birthstone earrings given to her years ago by her great-grandmother who I believed was already in heaven waiting to welcome her. Beside it was a framed picture of Krista elegantly dressed for her first prom, her only prom.

In one drawer of her desk we found twenty sheets of white typing paper that really puzzled me. Each sheet of paper had a collage of six or seven pictures of good-looking young men pasted on it. Obviously, they had been cut out of her *Teen* magazines. Several were pictures of her favorite star, Christian Slater. Why would anyone spend all that time cutting out and pasting pictures on sheets of paper if only to stick them in a drawer? I asked some of her girlfriends if they thought it was strange, and they confessed they did the same thing, just for fun, as a hobby.

When we cleaned out Krista's closet, we found two boxes of letters: a tall green box held possibly every note she had ever received from her girlfriends; a smaller, pink-flowered box contained letters from her boyfriend. Her girlfriends said they passed notes back and forth at school on a daily basis; they kept all of theirs, too. We decided to burn these personal items, as well as her diary, out of respect for her privacy. I knew if I kept them I would succumb to the temptation to read them.

Most of Krista's clothes were packed to donate to Goodwill or to be given to her friends. Some of the shirts we both wore I couldn't part with; wearing clothes we had picked out together made me feel close to her. To the bag of items to be burned, I added Krista's favorite pajamas, a pink flannel Esleep shirt and matching boxers, a gift from us on her 15th birthday. I couldn't picture anyone else wearing them.

When Darrell came back from burning the personal items, there were tears in his eyes.

"The pajamas," he whispered as we held each other, "no more goodnight hugs."

Opening a marble jewelry box on her shelf, we discovered a collection of key chains, five little plastic ones, the type that are commonly handed out at fair booths. One was a railroad crossing sign, with the words, "Stop, Look, Listen." Perhaps she had received it in Driver's Ed class.

As we sorted through her things, I told Darrell how sad it was that fifteen years of a child's life could fit neatly in a trunk and on a well-arranged bookshelf. He reminded me that these things are not what remains of our Krista. What does remain are every smile we shared, every vacation memory, all those special family moments, every laugh we enjoyed together, each goodnight hug and kiss, and especially the love we shared as her family: all of that was, *and is*, our Krista. Darrell is a very special man, a man of exceptional faith. As we shared memories and tears that day, God's love came to me through my husband.

If Krista had been our only child, I'm not sure the room would have been changed yet. Our surviving child had a lot to do with our decision to change the room so soon. We were concerned about avoiding setting up a shrine to our dead daughter. We wanted Jeff to know that we love him just as much as we love Krista, and that we are glad we are still a family.

When to confront your child's room is a personal decision. There is no right time to do it. I know parents who did it the day after the funeral. I know parents who did it two years after their child's death. And I know parents who still have the room intact, many years later, just as it was the day their child died. Personal circumstances dictate when a parent tackles this obstacle.

I would like to say things got better for us immediately after our decision to change the room, but they didn't. Instead, our pain deepened as we were forced to admit to ourselves that Krista was not coming home. As we packed up Krista's belongings, we also packed up our hopes that she might return. In order to begin our healing, we had to acknowledge our wound.

Jeff surprised us by asking if he could have Krista's old room. At his request we painted the room bright purple, teal and white, colors of a favorite NBA team, the Charlotte Hornets. Three months after Krista's death, the "room" had a new purpose.

---

The rock-n-roll sounds of "Jock Jam" blare from the stereo. Posters of cars and favorite sports stars are plastered sporadically on the walls, accentuating the room's new personality. Jeff lives here now, and the newly decorated room broadcasts his zest for life.

Across the hall is a modestly done reading room. Shades of pastel pink accented by rainbows give this room a quiet, reflective tone. Pictures of Krista and Jeff greet us as we enter the room. A trunk with a picture of a unicorn houses special belongings of our missing child. One bookshelf boasts huge photo albums and inspirational reading material. The other bookshelf displays reminders of precious memories. This room, too, has a purpose. The picture window, purposely void of curtains, allows the sunshine to warm us as we recline on a comfortable, blue-and-white striped mini-sofa, creating a pleasant place to sit and think, read and reflect. It is also a quiet retreat when the tears will not stop.

# THE MISSING PLATE

Our family had always made a special effort to eat supper together at the end of the day and make time to discuss the day's events. It was painful to set three plates at the table when there should have been four. I hated looking at Krista's empty chair. So, for awhile, we decided to forget about eating in the dining room and settled for meals in front of the TV to provide distraction. We also ate more meals out. Frozen pizzas or sandwiches in front of the TV and meals at restaurants replaced our usual supper routine for several months. When friends came to eat with us, mealtime was easier because their presence lessened the impact of the missing plate.

For a long time I didn't really feel like cooking. It was hard to make foods Krista liked when she couldn't be there to eat them. I threw out a box of shrimp I found in the freezer because it was our favorite meal to share when the men in the family were gone. I couldn't bear to look at it. I was angered by the dill spears and cream cheese for her pickle wrap snacks in the refrigerator. I threw them out, too. When I made a pumpkin pie for Darrell at his request about three months after the accident, I cried most of the day because it was her favorite dessert and she wouldn't be there to eat it.

Krista and I had shared a passion for chocolate. We had our own private stash hidden from the guys for those times when a woman just needs chocolate. For a while after she died, I lost my appetite for chocolate. When friends brought something chocolate because they knew it was my favorite, I ate it to be polite, but afterwards I was always nauseous. How could I eat chocolate when my daughter could no longer enjoy it?

Was throwing out food crazy? How bizarre some of the things can be that we find difficult to cope with! I had never before thought food was a major problem for people in grief. I wondered about my sanity when things like this were getting me down. When I finally got up the nerve to discuss mealtime at my grief support group, I was amazed and relieved to hear other stories of "food hangups" regarding a loved one's favorite foods. Perhaps we're all made a little mad by grief.

Adjusting to change takes time. Eventually, we were ready to eat regular meals again at home. Now I really do enjoy cooking when I have the time.

# RUNNING

Several weeks after Krista's death, we began what I call "running." We found it very difficult to be at home without her. We went to a lot of basketball games. Krista never liked sports, so it was one of the few places where it seemed bearable to go without her.

We wanted Jeff to be with us, but he needed to be with his friends. I'm sure he was "running" too. When our son was gone for an evening, it was even more imperative we not be left behind at home.

We ate out often at restaurants with leisurely service so it would be longer before we had to go home. Sometimes we drove to the Wal-Mart discount store ten miles away and walked around the store without buying anything, just for something to do, just to get out of the house. We were running away from home, trying to get away from the pain, but it followed us wherever we went.

Running was not a mistake for us. It was a survival technique. Escaping temporarily from the situation made it possible for us to get through the pain of those first months. We always had to face Krista's absence again when we came home, but I don't think I could have stood the pressure of having to face reality constantly during those first few months.

When we tired of "running," we had to stay home and feel the pain. Grief doesn't just go away. Maybe the pain of grief is like a cancer of the soul. Just as chemotherapy is used to destroy the cancer cells in the body and keep it from spreading, tears can purify the soul and allow the grieving heart to heal.

# TRAINS AND OTHER MONSTERS

One of the rooms in our house had been set up as a train room where my husband and son could work together on a special project just for fun. After our daughter's accident, we packed up all the trains and train memorabilia and stored them. There will be no more train shows for us.

I hate trains! Every time I hear a train whistle, or wait for a train at a crossing, or come across a train in a movie, book, or photo, I am faced with deep feelings of anger, sadness, and nostalgia. To me, trains are monsters of death. A train changed my life forever, robbing me of the future I had dreamed about with my child. Even the word "train" is a trigger that sets off a host of negative emotions within me.

Railroad crossings are plentiful in northeast Iowa. I cross at least one every time I leave the house in my car. Whenever I have to sit at a crossing waiting for a train to pass, I imagine myself backing up the car, stepping on the gas, and hitting the train at full speed. I want to go where Krista went. I want to feel what she felt. I want to stop hurting.

Krista did not want to die. She wanted to live. I know because she and I had discussed suicide. One of her friends was suicidal, and she worried about him. After her accident I told him he needed to remember how much Krista loved life, because it would make her very angry, and me, too, if he showed so little respect for life, that he would take his own.

The train is my enemy. In 1994, 615 people were killed in highway-rail grade crossing collisions. The newspapers print stories of lives devoured by these iron monsters. I refuse to feed their insatiable hunger.

Representatives from the railroad appeared at our door the Saturday after the tragedy. They were not welcome. I did not appreciate their presence. I listened unemotionally as they extended formal condolences on behalf of the railroad. They wanted us to know they would pay for the funeral. But that wouldn't bring back my daughter, would it?

The railroad men visited us again a week after the funeral. I knew they meant well, but it made me very uncomfortable to have them in our home. I mentioned the fact that others had died at the same unmarked crossing, yet in spite of pleas from area residents, no lights or gates had been installed. I asked how many people would have to die there before precautions would be deemed necessary. They informed me that it was not their responsibility; it was a decision of the state's Department of Transportation to determine which crossings required lights. They did not feel the railroad was liable.

Fog was another factor in Krista's accident. Every foggy night reminds me of the night she died. I asked why trains aren't grounded in the fog like airplanes. One of the men explained that only a handful of people are killed during an accident like our daughter's, whereas hundreds of people might be killed at once if a plane crashes because of the fog. I believe the trains should not have been allowed to run on the night our daughter died. Anyone who was driving on that road at that particular time would have met with disaster because the train was not visible in the thick fog. Airlines couldn't afford the liability if a plane crashed in the fog because so many lives would be lost. Since fewer lives are risked at railroad crossings, the people making the decisions apparently believe the potential for a fatal collision is an acceptable risk. Would they feel differently if the only life lost was that of their own son or daughter, brother or sister? Count on it!

Sometimes anger can be channeled appropriately. The parents of Derek Steva, the boy who was driving the car involved in Krista's accident, initiated a massive letter writing campaign directed to the Iowa Department of Transportation following the death of these three young people. Lights and gates were later installed at the intersection as a result of their pleas. However, there are hundreds of other crossings in the county which still have no safety systems. It would be too expensive to install such safety devices at all crossings. This one qualified only because of the number of lives lost there and the public outcry. Why is money so precious and human life so expendable?

Several months after Krista's death, we received a phone call from a lawyer in Colorado wanting to represent us in a lawsuit against the railroad. He specialized in these cases throughout the United States. When I asked if our lawsuit would have any effect on improving installation of crossing gates and lights throughout the area, he replied it would not. I asked if the money paid to us in a settlement would have any bearing on changing any railroad safety policies in the future; he admitted it would not. We told him we weren't interested. Why should we subject ourselves to the extra stress of a drawn-out legal battle which would accomplish nothing but money in our pockets? Not only would the lawsuit not bring back our daughter, but it would do nothing to prevent a similar tragedy.

If our daughter had been driving, we probably would have responded differently. Perhaps we would have believed we owed it to her to prove it was not just driver error that resulted in three deaths that foggy night. In those circumstances, we might have chosen to become involved in a lawsuit.

I believe most people who have had a loved one die have some trigger word associated with the death. The word may be "cancer," "fire," "alcohol," or "motorcycle"; or if the deceased had been murdered, the trigger word might be more specific, such as the name of a weapon or the name of the killer. I don't know how long these trigger words maintain power over us.

An acquaintance reminded us several months after Krista's death about an upcoming train show we might want to attend. When I informed her that we had packed up all of our model trains and were no longer interested in pursuing that interest, she pointed out that we were being irrational, that it was foolish to have such strong feelings toward an inanimate object. All of her children are still living.

My feelings are my own. No one can tell me how I should feel. I am grateful that my anger can be directed at an object rather than at a person.

Anger is a natural response to grief. I will not allow it to control my life, but I cannot deny its existence. Some days the anger is just there, welled up inside, ready to explode. During those times I'm not angry at anyone in particular, but everyone I encounter can probably sense my emotion. I'm just upset because Krista isn't here, and the fact of her death angers me. I tend to be a recluse when I'm angry, so usually my family members are the unfortunates forced to deal with it.

Finding an appropriate way to release the anger is difficult. Using energy exercising may afford some relief. I'm not very athletically inclined, so sports are not an effective way for me to relieve this excess energy.

One of the books I read suggested relieving the pent-up energy by breaking old dishes that were about to be discarded anyway. Since we live in the country, I didn't need to worry about anyone seeing my strange behavior, so I decided to try the suggestion. We have a fire pit in the back yard that adequately contained the shattering glass as I demolished the dishes, releasing the rage I had been repressing. When I returned to the scene later with a broom and dustpan to dispose of the evidence of my lunacy, I was actually laughing a little at the absurdity of what I had done.

We seem to have a short supply of laughter at our house these days. Have the monsters devoured it? *I miss the laughter.*

# WHAT ABOUT GOD?

When a tragedy occurs, one of the first questions asked is always, "What about God?" This was certainly true in our situation. Many people sought to comfort me by assuring me that our daughter's death was "God's will." In the beginning I believed them because it was the only way I could cope. Some even went so far as to hint that we would someday see Krista's death as a blessing to our future life in some way we were not yet aware of. I will never see Krista's death as a blessing. Her life was a great blessing. I know these remarks were made by well-meaning people trying to ease my pain, but my grief cannot be explained away.

Our minister made one visit to our home a couple of weeks after Krista's funeral. As we talked, I mentioned that I did not believe Krista's death was God's will, but I did believe God knew Krista was going to die that night. The minister disagreed with me, saying it was unlikely since we all have free will. He did not convince me. Although I believe human beings have been given free will and our decisions affect our lives, I believe God is very perceptive; I think He knows us well enough to know some of the decisions we will likely make. After all, He is God.

I must explain my concept of God. I do not give you this information to change your image of God. God is too big to fit into a neat little box with a label. Your vision of God is every bit as valid as mine. I share this information only as history, forty-three years of experiences that led me to my ideas about God at the time of Krista's death. God is a central character in my story. My reactions to death and life will differ from everyone else's reactions because of my particular faith journey.

What religion am I? I am a Christian. The unchanging constant in my journey is the belief that Jesus Christ was God in human form and that he died on the cross and rose from the dead, making eternal life a reality. I have many questions about God and heaven and eternal life, but I believe strongly in their existence. I have practiced my religion as a Lutheran, a Congregationalist, a Methodist. My faith is alive, and like all living things, continues to change.

My parents took me to Sunday School and we worshiped together in church. I do not remember a time when we did not go to church. I complained like any normal kid when I was forced to learn Bible verses--I never dreamed how important they would become later in my life. I was baptized and confirmed in the Lutheran church.

My godmother, Aunt Norrie, took her position seriously. She bought me my first Bible and my first hymnal, which I seldom used, and was present at all the major events in my life. She kept in contact with me on a regular basis even after I married and moved out of Wisconsin. She traveled a hundred miles to be with us for Krista's baptism and again for her confirmation. We talked often about God in an informal way, about his presence in our lives. She prayed for me often. I prayed for her occasionally.

Aunt Norrie never worked a full-time paid job in the years I knew her. She lived a life of service and kept busy with volunteer work. I proudly display one of her quilts in my living room. She designed it especially for Krista, to be given to her on her 25th birthday or her wedding day, whichever came first. Aunt Norrie died a year after Krista died. The lovingly crafted quilts she gave away and the flower gardens she planted and tenderly cared for are her legacy. Norrie was a giver. I loved my godmother. She loved hundreds.

When I graduated from high school, I attended a Lutheran college for one year. It was here I began to seriously question religion. The year was 1968. Racial tensions were a major issue at many colleges, and mine was no different. We went to chapel every day and prayed together as one people, but when the sun went down, an ugly side of campus life emerged. Black students had their rooms broken into; lipsticked graffiti on their mirrors spoke of hate. They walked the campus in small groups and carried knives. My eyes were opened to hypocrisy. In chapel, we preached love; some practiced hate. I stopped going to church. I made plans to transfer to a public college. I was idealistic and inexperienced. I could not separate the actions of a few from the church as a whole.

That summer when I returned home I refused to attend church with my family. I was over eighteen; my parents did not insist.

In late August, only a couple weeks before I was to begin studying at a new university, I ran into a girlfriend from high school in one of our hometown stores. Rhonda looked great. She seemed genuinely happy, and I wondered if there was a new man in her life. I invited her to stop by my parents' house so we could visit. I listened to Rhonda talking about school, working, and her volunteer activities. Finally, I had to ask.

"You seem so happy. Is there a new guy you're not telling about?"

She laughed. "No, not really."

"Well, something's different."

Rhonda shared the story of her work with the campus ministry, the fun she had with her Christian friends, the excitement of her volunteer projects. I was jealous. I felt something was missing from my life.

When I started college that fall at the state university in Platteville, I visited several churches until I found one that felt comfortable, and I began attending regularly again. While Darrell and I were dating, we selected a church together. This time I was a Congregationalist.

Darrell and I broke up the summer before my junior year. Things had been getting serious between us, and I was afraid of commitment. What if I married the wrong man? At my urging, we decided to date other people for awhile. After about six weeks, I missed Darrell and wondered if the breakup had been a mistake. I knew he was dating someone else. He didn't want to date me again unless there was a commitment, unless we planned to get married.

One Sunday morning in October, I attended the Congregational church in Platteville where Darrell and I had worshiped together when we were dating. It was the first time I had gone there since our breakup. As I waited for church to begin, I said a silent prayer for guidance. I asked God to give me a sign if Darrell was the right one for me, before he found someone else and it was too late. I opened my eyes to see Darrell walk alone into the pew in front of me and sit down. I never had any doubts about marrying him after that. My prayer was answered swiftly, directly. That was the day I knew for certain God answers prayer.

After being married in the Lutheran church of my home congregation, we started our life together by searching for a church home in Dubuque, Iowa. We didn't want to be just members of a church; we wanted to be participants of a community of faith. A class at the Lutheran church was very helpful to us. It was especially designed for people with no formal religious background, people who previously considered themselves nonbelievers. In attending it we made the decision to reaffirm our confirmation vows, this time understanding their meaning more clearly. We participated in an evangelism outreach program that was instrumental in strengthening our own faith.

We have had five church homes since Dubuque. All of them were centered on the fundamental belief in Jesus Christ which is the main element of our faith. We selected each not because of its label, but because it was the most personally inviting to us of those available in the area. Some of our church homes have been better than others. We have come to the conclusion that the church is not a minister, or a building, or a set of theological rules. The church is people. The quality of a church is determined by the way in which members of the church care for each other, for their community, for their neighbors of all denominations.

After Krista's death, we re-evaluated all areas of our life, including our religion. St. Paul Lutheran Church had always felt much more stiff and formal than our previous church homes. We thought seriously about changing churches at the time. It would have been easier than returning to the same church without Krista.

Why didn't we change? Because when we were in excruciating pain, our church members were there for us. The congregation cared for us physically and emotionally. They supplied us with chicken soup, rolls, brownies, hamburger casseroles. An elderly couple came to visit several weeks after Krista's death, and we talked of love and pets and loss. A young mother brought boxes of books and asked if there was anything she could do to help. Remembrances made me feel less alone--flowers on Valentine's Day, a gold necklace with a "K" charm for Mother's Day, a card on the anniversary of Krista's death, all sent anonymously from my secret sister in the church. The warmth in the hearts of our fellow church members brought us God's comfort to dry our tears. How could we leave them?

I know many people who quit going to church after a tragedy occurred in their lives. I always assumed they quit attending because they blamed God for their circumstances. Now I wonder whether they thought it was God who let them down, or whether they just became disillusioned with the church itself because the people of their congregation did not minister to them appropriately in their time of need. Love prompts us to take action to comfort those in our midst who mourn, whatever the loss might be--an illness, a fire, a job, financial security, a reputation, a marriage, a loved one. We are His hands in this world.

Some of Krista's friends were angry because they felt God should have saved her, that He should have arranged for the car to have a flat tire before they reached the train or somehow prevented the tragedy from occurring. My response is that we are not puppets on a string. I don't believe God plays those kinds of games with us. Yes, He could have intervened. There could have been a miracle. I believe strongly in miracles. But God did not intervene. I don't know why. Instead, events took their course, and our little girl died.

Krista's birth had been a miracle in my eyes. Darrell and I were married seven years before Krista was born. We had wanted children sooner, but nothing happened. I remember the sadness and disappointment I felt each month during those years of waiting, when I did not become pregnant as I'd hoped. First I prayed I would have children; later my prayer changed to a request for God to help me accept the fact that I would not have children of my own and help me find another way to enjoy children. I continued to be involved with children professionally, as an elementary teacher, and informally, through work with our church youth. Then came the miracle, Krista Lin Kifer arrived on January 17, 1979, a beautiful, healthy baby girl.

I know it is common to be angry at God when tragedy strikes. Almost everyone I have ever talked to who is missing a dead child speaks about their anger at God. But our situation is different. How could I be angry with the God who gave me this beautiful miracle?

My God's plan is for life, not death. I don't believe our death date is pre-arranged conveniently before we are born. If that were true, none of our decisions would matter; life would have no meaning. How could it ever be God's will for people to die horrible deaths by murder, accident, disease, war! Good people and bad people share a common enemy--death. We all die. Some will die sooner than others, before they have a chance to accomplish all that we believe was intended for them. Death is not fair. We become vividly aware of this fragile quality of life when a child dies.

I don't know why my daughter happened to be in a particular place at the wrong time when a train ended her life. Would it matter if I knew why? No reason would be good enough to satisfy me. When Krista drew her final breath, God was there with her. His presence makes a difference to me. She is not alone, never has been, never will be.

I can feel God's love in those who reach out to me in friendship and compassion. I sense His presence as I listen to His Word. I am reminded that He keeps promises as I witness a rainbow.

What about God? The God I worship is powerful. He doesn't need anyone to make excuses for Him when bad things happen. He keeps His promises. He promised to be with me always, to be with Krista always, and He is. He didn't promise that my daughter wouldn't die. He did promise those who believe, though they die, yet shall they live--eternal life. *Death is not the final word.*

# HER BIRTHDAY

Only a month after Krista's death, we had to face the first missed birthday. Every bereaved parent I've talked to lists this as one of the hardest days of the year, and not just the first year, but all the succeeding years as well.

Birthdays had been big celebrations at our home. We decorated with crepe paper, made signs, and ate birthday cake. It was the one day of the year that belonged uniquely to each of us. Presents were opened first thing in the morning because we were too excited to wait all day. The birthday person chose the favorite foods to be served at our special dinner. When the kids grew older, they had another party with their friends in addition to the family celebration.

---

Krista would have been sixteen today. She planned to have either her Dad or me take her to Decorah to get her driver's license. She had asked months ago to have the car tonight. She was so excited about the new adventures she would have once she secured the coveted driver's license. But she's not here today. There are no presents, no cake, no celebration.

---

My mother had come to spend the day with us. It helped having her here, knowing how much she loves Krista, too. Mom gave me a "pinky" ring with Krista's birthstone. She and I went to the cemetery early in the day and placed roses on Krista's grave. The flowers were not for Krista to see, but rather a reminder of the love we shared with the special person who used that earthly body for fifteen years. We cried because this wasn't the way her

16th birthday was supposed to be. We cried for all the other birthdays she'll never have. Her friends had been to the cemetery before us and left notes and flowers. (Thank you for remembering.)

Jeff, Mom and I, and one of Krista's friends, spent the morning together at our house. We joined Darrell for lunch, seeking comfort in our common grief. The old phrase "the more, the merrier" definitely did not apply.

I ended this awful day with a silent prayer:

> *Lord, this day is finally done. Night has come. Refresh us Lord. Grant us peace that we might sleep. You know how heavy my heart is, how great my sorrow today. Your Son died, too. But He was coming home to you. I am separated from my child for much too long... Help me get out of bed tomorrow. Help me face the future, one day at a time. I can't do it without you. I am weak; You are strong. Thank you for carrying me today. Amen.*

I thought about the future and all the birthdays we wouldn't be celebrating in the years ahead. Will her father and I be the only ones that remember this special day, the only ones that take a flower to her grave? Others will return to a normal life, which is to be expected, and this date will not be important to them.

As we passed Krista's birthday a second time, there were two flowers on her grave, a red rose from Darrell, a pink rose from me. Krista would have been seventeen on the seventeenth, her "golden" birthday. Will we mourn again on the day she should be turning eighteen and becoming a legal adult? What about when she should be twenty-one and perhaps graduating from college or getting married? Darrell and I will count the years silently, and no one else will hear. We will comfort each other as best we can because she is still our child, even though we cannot see her.

*Since we cannot give Krista a gift on her birthday, we give a donation in her memory to charities that serve children. Anything we do to help other children seems to lift our spirits.*

As this book goes to press, we have just passed the fourth birthday without Krista. For the first time this year Darrell and I went to her grave together on the morning of her birthday to deliver a single pink rose. It doesn't get easier. The day will always be a special day; we will never forget.

# FOR BETTER, FOR WORSE

Darrell and I met at a "grasser" when we were both students attending the University in Platteville, Wisconsin. I had never heard of a grasser before that night. The Town of Platteville had adopted a twenty-one-year-old drinking age even though legal drinking age in Wisconsin at that time was eighteen. Resourceful college kids skirted the problem by organizing beer parties known as grassers held in country pastures.

Fliers advertising these outdoor events were abundant at girls' dorms. My girlfriend and I had made plans to attend a get-acquainted party at the union sponsored by a campus Christian group on Thursday night. The flier in the lobby announced an all-school grasser to be held the same night: Bonfire. Live Music. Hot dogs and Beer included. Price: Guys--$5.00, Girls--Free. A sketchy map on the bottom showed the location in a pasture two miles from town.

The price was right. But how would we get there? Mary Jo was the social butterfly on our dorm floor. She was resourceful. She could get us a ride. At Mary Jo's urging, our trip to the union was cancelled, exchanged for an opportunity to attend the major grasser event.

We never made it to the all-school grasser. We ended up at a smaller version on top of the "M," two miles in the other direction. Platteville's university had begun as a mining school in the early 1900s. The large "M" built out of limestone was a college landmark, still serving a purpose every spring when lit up with torches in celebration of the annual Miner's Ball.

It took about ten minutes for us to climb to the top of the "M." No band. No hot dogs. No bonfire. Just beer and chips. We were at a private party for about twenty people. I was not happy. Thanks a lot, Mary Jo.

I spotted a deserted blue blanket near the edge of the hill and sat down alone to survey the situation.

"Can I join you?"

All I could discern in the dark about the man behind the voice was that he was very tall and had dark hair. I loved his deep voice.

"Doesn't matter to me. It's not my blanket." I was in my "Men are Pigs" phase.

"I know. It's mine."

He laughed as he sat beside me, identifying himself as Darrell Kifer. We exchanged the usual college get-acquainted small talk. Where are you from? What class are you in? What is your major? Etcetera. I was not particularly warm. There seemed to be an even ratio of boys to girls and I was annoyed by the setup. He asked if I wanted to go to a movie on Sunday night.

"Okay". Then I added, "But I don't believe in kissing until you're engaged.

Silence.

"Pick you up at 7:00."

"Right."

After the hard time I had given Darrell, I expected to be stood up, so I didn't bother getting ready for our date. I was in my room reading Sunday night about 7:15 when the phone rang.

"Carol?"

"Yes. Who is this?"

"It's Darrell. I'm downstairs."

Twenty minutes later after washing and blow-drying my hair and applying makeup I arrived in the lobby to meet Darrell. He was still there, waiting patiently.

We talked very little on our first date, just smiled a lot and exchanged shy glances over cherry cokes after the movie. As we kissed goodnight, I had to ask: "Why did you keep this date?"

"I like challenges." He had a great smile.

When I returned to my dorm room, I picked up the pen lying on my cluttered desk and scribbled a notation on the calendar under the block for September 18, 1969: "Met Darrell Kifer."

We were married in June 1972. We still have the blanket we met on. I married my best friend. I loved him. He is still my best friend. I love him more.

Darrell and I are opposites. He likes plain vanilla ice cream. I like turtle sundaes with extra nuts. I am punctual. He is always late. We hold opposing views on many issues. I think life would be boring if we agreed about everything. Life at our house includes confrontation. It also includes respect for another opinion.

Darrell has always been an optimist. He expects everything to go smoothly, to work out. He does not anticipate problems. He lives life one day at a time and faces life's difficulties as temporary obstacles to be dealt with to the best of one's ability before moving on. He has many dreams. I am a worrier. I anticipate that things will go wrong unless we take precautions. Sometimes I find his views idealistic and accuse him of being unrealistic.

I envy Darrell's ability to cope and his easy-going manner. Everyone likes Darrell. He strikes up a conversation with a stranger at an airport in Chicago or on the beaches of Mexico and within five minutes they have discovered a common acquaintance somewhere in the United States. He loves people and sees the good in each of them.

I admire and respect this man I have lived with for twenty-four years. I have seen him cry three times since I've known him--once when we were dating, and the other times for Krista. Often, I see the tears in his eyes, but he seldom allows their release.

We are two individuals who chose to journey through life together, supporting each other in love "for better or worse." This was definitely the "worse."

Darrell and I are the kind of people who don't need parties or throngs of people around us to be happy. We enjoy doing things as a couple. I thought Darrell and I could handle anything together. But when Krista died, it soon became apparent that providing adequate support for each other was impossible because we were equally devastated. For us to lean on each other for sole support during this time would have been like expecting two blades of grass to support a housing structure. The strength wasn't there.

Although we talked about Krista often and communicated our feelings, we needed support from other people. When I had a really bad day, I hated to burden Darrell and bring him down if he was having a good day. Talking to someone about my feelings was a necessary release for me.

Many of the grief books I read gave statistics on the high divorce rate for parents whose child has died. I found those statistics very frightening--90% divorce within ten years. My own parents divorced after thirty-five years of marriage and Darrell's parents after twenty-five years. I feared divorce was a possibility.

---

"A lot of people get divorced after they lose a child. Please, Darrell, don't let that happen to us," I whispered one night in the darkened bedroom. "I can't lose you, too."

"It'll be all right. We'll make it. I love you."

Was he really so sure?

---

In the two years since Krista's death, I have grown to understand that our grief is not the same. Although we both loved Krista with all our hearts, we grieve in very different ways. Mothers and fathers have different relationships with their children. Darrell was the protector. I was the nurturer. We have different issues to deal with. And men do grieve differently than women. Through the books I read and information I received in grief support groups, I was finally able to understand this concept. No matter how much a man and woman love each other, grief is an individual journey.

I want to share with you the day our two minds became one. That was a rare occurrence.

It was our second spring without Krista. We had been at one of Jeff's track meets in Postville, ten miles from home, at which Jeff set a new seventh grade school record in the 400 meter dash. We had two cars with us because I had come from home and Darrell had come directly from the office.

"See you at home."

On the way I decided to stop at the grocery store in Postville to get ten pounds of hamburger for the freezer. Their meat was especially flavorful, and I didn't get to Postville often--this was a once-every-six-months kind of event.

I also decided to stop at Krista's grave on the way home. I had noticed a cement crew at the cemetery earlier in the week and wanted to see if perhaps the monument for Derek, the oldest of the teenagers who died in the accident, had arrived. When I turned into the cemetery, I saw Darrell at the top of the hill standing in front of Krista's grave. It was obvious from his stance that he was praying. I wondered how often he came here.

We had come here together on Memorial Day and only a couple times after church. On Krista's birthday I knew Darrell had been here before me because of the red rose he'd left behind. This was the first time we'd both been here by chance.

We shared a hug at Krista's grave, then walked together, holding hands, to see Derek's freshly installed headstone. When I read the farewell letter from his parents engraved on it, I thought of all the parents left behind.

Darrell broke the silence.

"Meet you at home. Is there room in the freezer? I stopped in Postville and picked up ten pounds of hamburger. Why are you smiling?"

# WHO UNDERSTANDS MY LOSS?

My husband and I shared a common loss; our daughter's death had left us in a world of shattered dreams. Darrell lived in my world where life was unfair and heartache changed life into a constant struggle for survival.

One of the most difficult aspects of grief is the immense feeling of isolation from the rest of the world. I felt different from everyone else. *Disconnected* is the word that best describes me in the early stages of my grief.

I became a voyeur. I would watch mothers and daughters shopping together or talking together over a restaurant meal and take mental note of how normal their lives seemed to be. They were living the life I once had. I didn't feel this world was real. I wasn't part of the picture. I felt like the narrator in a book who has inside information the characters don't possess as they continue the daily business of living. I wondered if they had any idea how quickly it could all change.

I stopped participating in community groups I belonged to. Nothing interested me. Nothing seemed important. I withdrew from what I perceived as the world of normal people.

Sometimes when I went into a store, I received a casual greeting such as "How about this weather? Is it warming up out there any?"

I felt like shouting, "What difference does it make? It's only weather. Don't you know my daughter is dead?" But I restrained myself, answering in small talk, the language of strangers.

I understand now the value of the age-old custom of wearing black when in mourning. It is a custom seldom observed by anyone in our country these days. When grieving, it is frustrating to be treated as though everything were fine and to be required to act as though life were normal. Perhaps if we wore black, others would recognize the fact that we were in mourning and not expect so much of us. Our dark-colored clothing would be an outward manifestation of the fact that we are "different" at this time.

Before Krista died I had a number of misconceptions about bereaved parents. I remember feeling uncomfortable in the presence of Kris, the mother of a deceased classmate of Krista's. When I noticed this woman at baseball games or in the store, I had avoided her. I was afraid of saying the wrong thing. I was afraid seeing me with my child would remind her of her loss, and add to her grief. Perhaps I felt a little guilty that my family was intact and hers was not. Seeing her reminded me that my own child could die, too, and I didn't want to think about that. I know now I was wrong to avoid Kris, because I've experienced similar responses from other parents. Avoidance hurts. I have apologized to her. She understands that ignorance, not lack of compassion, caused my behavior. Ironically, I now seek Kris out often just to visit. I find her presence comforting. She has survived the same heartache. We can talk.

Friends and relatives loved and cared about me, but could they understand the depth of my loss? Discussions with other parents whose children had died became a crucial part of our grieving process. Our common sadness, despair, guilt, anxiety, and loneliness could be confessed and accepted by these partners in pain. Even our tears and strange visions were not reacted to with shock or disbelief. These people understood because they had been there, too.

An older man I had previously known only slightly, as a business acquaintance, shared the story of his teenage son's death following a routine tonsillectomy. Twin thirteen-year-old boys had entered the hospital together for the surgery, but one twin received an overdose of pain medication following the operation and died. The hospital was negligent--human error had taken an innocent child's life. The tragedy he spoke of took place twenty-five years before. Although he had eight children, seven of whom are still living, he misses the son who isn't here.

The first question asked by strangers when they meet a bereaved parent, is often "Do you have other children?" There is always a sigh of relief when they learn that we do. People seem to believe that the more children you have left alive, the quicker you will get over your loss. This is another popular misconception.

A mother visited us in our home a few days after Krista's death and shared her story. Waiting joyously for her twenty-year-old son's arrival home after two years of service in the armed forces, she received a phone call the day he was to return. Her son had just been killed in a motorcycle accident. She has a daughter, but will always miss her only son.

Our community had a number of children die within a three-year period, and many of the local students were directly affected by the deaths. After Krista and the other two teenagers died in a common accident, the guidance counselor at our local school organized special six-week counselling sessions, one for bereaved parents and one for bereaved siblings and friends. Some of those attending had faced the loss of a child more than ten years prior.

We heard the story of a four-year-old boy who was eating supper with his family when he collapsed with a brain aneurysm. His parents had no warning before his body failed. The woman sharing this story had lost her son almost twenty years before, and her continued participation in this formal support group helped those of us with recent losses. She acknowledged what our friends whose children were all living did not understand--that you don't get over it, you learn to live with it.

The story repeats itself again and again. I used to think a child's death was a rare occurrence. Now I know it is a common tragedy. But, like all tragedies, its existence becomes real only when it affects us directly. Realizing others have lived with this loss and are still living with it, we are given hope we will be able to do likewise.

Support groups are not all alike. When the school-sponsored support group disbursed following the six-week sessions, I searched for another group. I secured the address for Compassionate Friends, a national support group that focuses on the loss of a child, and had my name put on the mailing list of the nearest chapter. Since that group was seventy miles away, I never made it to the meetings, but I did receive their monthly newsletter of stories and poems that echoed my sentiments, making me feel less alone.

I questioned other bereaved parents I had met about the groups they had attended. There was one group within forty miles that was designed specifically for grieving parents. However, after a couple sessions, I determined it was not helpful to me because of their tendency to focus only on the loss, which made me feel worse, not better. I wanted tips for survival. Compassion was important, but in itself, not enough; I wanted hope. After shopping around, attending several different groups, I found one I felt comfortable with.

Later I joined a mixed group that included both those who had children die and those who were grieving for spouses or other relatives. Although I wanted to talk to someone with a similar loss, hearing about the struggles of women whose spouses had died made me aware that my still having Darrell with me was a blessing. Widows listened to my stories and seemed thankful to have all their children still living. I participated in a formal support group for about a year on a regular basis. By then I had developed some close relationships with other bereaved mothers, and received support through my communications with them on an informal basis. We continue to talk about our children, listen to each other's irrational activities, and remember each other on special days.

Whenever I read a newspaper account or hear a news story about a child's death, I feel compelled to communicate with that mother. Sometimes distance allows me only to send a card and letter, or make a phone call to a stranger; other times I am able to go to the house and extend my sympathy in person. I don't worry about what I will say. I go only to be there, to tell them I'm sorry, my child died, too, and I know how it hurts. Often I leave a book behind with my phone number. The parents seldom call. The book gives me an excuse to visit again months later and let them know someone still remembers and cares. I want to help others the way so many helped me. I do it out of compassion for these parents, but I also do it for selfish reasons. I still hurt. Sharing the pain helps us both.

The love connection continues when a loved one dies. Extending this love to others allows us to feel connected again in this world, if only for a few precious minutes.

# THE DEATHDAY

Remember all the decisions and planning you did before the child's birthday to ensure the party and the presents would be just right? It wasn't a one-day process, but was instead a greatly anticipated occasion that you prepared in advance to celebrate. Just as we once celebrated each birthday with gladness when our child was alive, we now seem destined to mourn the approaching deathday as we remember how long it has been since our child died.

During the weeks immediately preceding the first anniversary of Krista's death, I became increasingly agitated and had a great deal of trouble sleeping. Whereas time had been almost irrelevant to me during the preceding eleven months, as December ninth approached I began to find myself dreading the passing of each day.

---

I've been waking up nights a lot lately, hearing all those damn trains go by. It creates flashbacks to the night of Krista's accident. I can feel it happening all over again. My heart is pounding wildly. I sweat profusely in spite of the winter cold. The pain in my chest, arms and neck has returned. It's so hard to live in the present, to accept what *is* instead of *what should have been*. As it gets closer to the anniversary of Krista's death, I have an impending fear of loss. My mind wants to turn back the hands of time and do December 9, 1994, all over again with a different ending. I am in a state of panic wherein I need desperately to act, but I'm not sure what I'm supposed to be doing. It's as though when that date arrives--December 9, 1995--my last chance to change the reality of this past year will vanish.

Intellectually, I know I never possessed the power to change any of it. What happened is real. But emotionally I still can't accept the permanence of Krista's death.

---

December 9, 1995, has arrived. A year ago today at this time I still had a beautiful daughter to hug. A year ago tonight she went to stay at a friend's house and she never came home...

I miss Krista so much. I still see the sweet smile on her face. It is so difficult not to be able to put my arms around her and hold her tight.

We've somehow survived a whole year without our Krista. I really didn't think it was possible. I remember commenting when I read about other children's deaths in the newspaper prior to her death: "How can those parents go on? That's the one thing I could never live with." I'd said it more than once. I guess we never know what we *can* live with, or what we *will have to live with* until it happens.

# KRISTA'S FRIENDS

We enjoyed having teenagers at our home. Krista's friends were always welcome. Almost every weekend she had a girlfriend stay overnight. Some of her friends jokingly called us "Mom" and "Dad." We loved that.

The first couple months after Krista's death, her friends visited us often. They needed to talk about their loss. We needed to hear that she was missed. We attempted to support each other as we grieved. The teenagers showed genuine concern for us, and initially, their presence was very comforting. One girl even baked Christmas cookies for us.

I loved Krista's friends, but it seemed strange having them at our house without her. Listening to stories about the new experiences her friends were having became increasingly difficult. I waited eagerly for their visits, then cried for hours after they left because it made Krista's absence so unbearable.

The frequency of the teenagers' visits gradually dwindled. Her ex-boyfriend and closest girlfriend kept in touch with us for about six months. But the time came when we felt it was better for her friends and for us to admit that without Krista, we were part of each other's past. The bond had been broken.

I still miss her friends. I think about them often. Many of her classmates have jobs now, and occasionally I run into them in unexpected places. The normalcy of their lives is a constant reminder of how different life has become for our family.

What is Krista doing right now? I wonder about her adventures as she explores the final frontier I believe waits for all of us someday--life beyond the grave. What is it like? Why was I left behind?

# WHERE IS SHE?

My daughter died. I did not lose her. I know exactly where she is. The remains of her earthly body lie in a grave at the edge of town. Ironically, the train that ended her life passes by several times each day and night, whistling its "good-bye" over and over. But Krista does not hear it. She is dead.

I believe Krista now lives in heaven. I am not sure of the nature of heaven. Is it a place or is it a state of being? What about reincarnation?

We each have our own vision of heaven. To me, heaven means being in God's constant presence. I can feel that presence in my heart as I live that portion of eternal life that is spent here in the present. Does learning continue in our new life in its most perfect form, without the distractions we face on earth?

When I find myself feeling depressed about all the things Krista never experienced in this life because she died so young, I try to imagine the new life she's experiencing.

As a mother my main concern has always been for the safety of my children. I would have given anything to have saved my child; I would have chosen to die in her place if I'd been given a choice. We don't get to make those choices. Death comes on its own schedule, its own terms. I find comfort in my belief that Krista is now safe in God's presence. A mother can bear any pain when she knows her child is okay.

I have painted a picture in my mind of our reunion in heaven. Time becomes irrelevant. Whether we meet again today or fifty years from now, Krista will just turn around and I'll be there. We'll know each other instantly no matter how long we have been separated. Perhaps we won't meet as mother and daughter, but as two souls connected by love, children of our Heavenly Father.

I am not afraid to die. I remember my grandmother's unwavering sense of eternal life.

---

When Grandpa died of cancer after a lengthy illness, I was only in fifth grade. In those days children didn't attend funerals. Shortly after his death, Grandma moved into an apartment on the second floor of my parents' home. She had two small rooms and a bathroom; the two remaining bedrooms on that floor were also occupied, one by my sister and me, the other by my brother. Having Grandma nearby was a blessing. She became a second mother to all three of us. Grandma was my confidante. Although she had many children and grandchildren, our relationship was extra special.

Grandma knew God's word well. She read from her Bible daily, and her devotional booklet, "Portals of Prayer," was always on the table by her bed. She was confident about her Lutheran religious beliefs and enjoyed discussing religion. When Jehovah's Witnesses knocked on our door, my parents were never interested in talking to them, so I'd just send them on up to Grandma. Although she didn't agree with their beliefs, she admired them for their commitment to preach the Word to all. I wonder if she ever converted any of them.

Grandma also liked to discuss politics. She made use of TV and newspapers to keep informed of current events. She had an opinion on everything, but never tried to force her ideas on others. She was never judgmental about other people. "Only God can judge" was her motto. She spent her time sewing, baking, and serving others rather than gossiping.

Grandma loved life. The mischievous sparkle in her eye let us know she was never too old to have fun.

I remember her listening to loud music and twisting with my friends and me one New Year's Eve when I was in high school. How I loved that woman! I wanted to be like her when I grew up.

Several years after I was married, one November, Grandma came to stay with Darrell and me for a few days at our home in Waukon, Iowa. We went shopping downtown. I surprised her by buying the dressy red patent-leather pumps she was admiring in the store window. She confessed that she'd always wanted a pair of shoes like that, but knew people would laugh to see an old lady like her in red shoes. I convinced her that at her age she could wear whatever she wanted. Grandma looked very stylish in her red shoes when we went to church together that Sunday.

Before she left to return to my parents' home, Grandma gave me a handmade baby quilt for my hope chest. I confided to her my concern that Darrell and I would be unable to have kids.

"You will," she said, winking. "Soon."

When I mentioned that I had her name in our Christmas present exchange and was working on a special project for her gift, Grandma informed me that she would not be alive for Christmas, that she would be joining my grandfather, Amon, in heaven. "Don't talk like that."

She put her arms around me, smiling. "Carol, I'm not afraid to die. I've had a good life. I've spent so many Christmases without your Grandpa. I've been talking to God, you know. He knows I'm ready to go."

"What? Are you sick? What's the matter?"

"I'm fine. When I go, it will be quick. Heaven will be an adventure." Her characteristic wink let me know it was all right.

I continued to work on the ceramic nativity set I was painting for her Christmas gift. In late November, only a couple weeks after her visit, my mother called to say that

Grandma had died in her sleep. Hers was the first funeral I ever attended. I was twenty-five years old. I remember nothing about that day except feeling embarrassed by tears I could not control.

---

When we are separated from someone we love by death, faith cannot take away the pain, but it can make it possible for us to go on living as people of hope. Thank you, Grandma, for sharing your faith.

Based upon my experiences and resulting beliefs, I have made an intellectual decision about where my daughter is. But on an emotional level, I continue to search for Krista. I see her face across a crowded gym, catch a glimpse of the back of her head as we pass a group of teenagers walking to school or gathering at the movie theater, hear her laughter from the crowded booth in the other room at Pizza Hut. It's all a cruel hoax fashioned out of grief. She is not here.

# OUR SURVIVING SON

Jeff was born on April Fool's Day, ten months after we sold all our baby items, convinced we would never have a second child. We love our son as we love Krista, completely, unconditionally, always, because he is ours.

Strangers remark about Jeff's beautiful, thick auburn hair. When he was a toddler, this was usually followed by the comment that he should have been a girl. I smiled at this observation because he has always been "all boy". Our freckle-faced son was less than a year old when he broke his arm. He and his sister had been riding horseback double on Dad as he crawled around on all fours. When they fell off, Krista landed on top of Jeff. Jeff whimpered for perhaps half a minute, but didn't seem seriously hurt. Several days later I realized he was using his left hand instead of his right to pick up things, so I took him to the doctor to have his arm x-rayed. It was broken in two places. I felt like the world's stupidest mother, but he had shown no sign of pain.

He climbed window sills before he walked.

At two he wanted to be a fireman. One day I was forced to quickly excuse myself from a phone conversation in response to the sound of breaking glass, followed promptly by a loud, "Oh, oh" in another room.

I entered the room angrily, prepared to deal with the mess caused by his "terrible two" rambunctiousness. I surveyed the wreckage of the pole lamp that had previously stood beside the couch. The two golden globes had been snapped off completely by the impact of his Snoopy tennis shoes as he slid down the pole. Innocent blue eyes looked up at me, peeking out from under the rim of an oversized red plastic fireman's hat.

"That darn thing. We got to get a new fire pole, Mom."

My anger was replaced by a slow smile that erupted into laughter as I reached out to hug my uninjured son. The world was a playground for exploration, every object a potential toy for his vivid imagination.

Jeff was eleven when Krista died. I was amazed by the support he received from his peers. Since they had no preconceived notions about grief to interfere with their friendship, they were able to continue their relationship with him on a separate level, allowing him a sense of stability in contrast to a rapidly changing home environment. His friends kept him busy, going places, doing things, moving. He needed activity and they supplied it. He has learned valuable lessons about friendship, about the importance of just being there.

Six months after Krista's death, Jeff confided a concern that he was not a good friend.

"Mom, do you remember when Emily's Mom died?" Emily was a classmate of Jeff's whose mother died of a prolonged illness three months before Krista's death.

"Yes. Why?"

"I didn't go to the funeral or anything. She's my friend. I should have been there. Why didn't I go?"

I told Jeff he probably didn't know before Krista died how painful it is when someone you love dies, or how much you need your friends. I shared my regret for not being with my mother when her father died. I was twenty-two. Mom needed me and I wasn't there for her. I didn't know about the hurt. We need to forgive ourselves for our ignorance. Both of us will be there the next time someone needs us. Jeff has learned compassion.

Jeff at thirteen is ruggedly good looking with broad shoulders and real muscles. Where does this physique come from? His father and I are strictly non-athletic types.

Sports are his passion, and he is reasonably good at all of them.

"Someday," he tells me, "I'm going to play professional ball--maybe basketball, football, and baseball. I'll get season tickets for you and Dad."

I am glad he has dreams.

He has become very self-confident. He is a leader, not a follower. Sometimes when we talk on the phone, I don't recognize his voice right away. He has a man's voice now, and I still expect to hear a child.

Our phone rings continuously, sometimes boys, more often girls, searching for our son. Some of his best friends are girls. He has always been very socially oriented and since his sister's death he needs his friends even more.

I rejoice because Jeff is here. We can see his clear blue eyes and impish smile, hug him when his friends are not watching, hear his laughter and corny jokes, and smell the cheese sandwiches he claims are his specialty when he cooks supper.

We dream with him about his future. But the fear is always there. What if he has no future? What if history repeats itself? What if something happens to him?

I believe most parents worry about the possibility their child could be fatally injured, but deep down they feel it can't happen to them. I know it can happen to us.

I do not want to be obsessive in my concern for this remaining child, but it is a very difficult struggle. My experience has proven life is not fair. So I worry, because that's what mothers do. Intellectually, I know life is either an adventure to be experienced, or it is nothing. I force myself to let Jeff go, let him grow, because that's what mothers must do.

Jeff is a constant reminder to me that today is worth living. I ponder how much more difficult life must be for parents who have been left behind with no surviving children. I say a special prayer for those who have no child to hold, that they might receive extra servings of love from friends and family.

# HOW CAN I HELP MYSELF?

I have never considered myself to be a strong person. I wasn't born with the triumphant spirit of Jackie Kennedy, able to handle life's tragedies with a sense of grace and style. I am the voice of the cowardly lion in the *Wizard of Oz* who has only the tiniest bit of courage, enough strength to ask for help because I know I can't do it alone.

I began my search for help by reading all the books I could locate on grief. Books by psychologists and grief counselors described the stages of grief so I could understand the process involved in coping with loss. One piece of advice that was fairly consistent in these books was the warning against making major changes in our lives at this time. We fought our inclination to move away, find new jobs, a new house. Our urge to run away was strong, but realistically, our problems would have followed us wherever we went.

Jeff had returned to school the day after the funeral. Darrell had returned to work after a week. I had intended to stay home for a couple weeks, but had ended up going back after ten days. Because the train that killed Krista passed by our house several times each day, I needed to escape its menacing whistles. Darrell and I each maintained our present jobs for a full year after Krista's death. It was important to have some stability in our lives.

Books about near-death experiences reinforced my belief that death was not the end of life, but only the beginning. I did not agree with everything I read, but many of the materials provided thought-provoking concepts.

I also concentrated much of my reading time on memoirs written by other parents about the loss of their own children. I needed to know someone else had hurt this bad and survived. I discovered there were lots of questions, but no definite answers.

Each person's loss was unique. Each person's grief was different. There is no right way to grieve. The common theme of the memoirs was the realization that death is permanent. We cannot change it. Survival involves adjusting to the absence of our special child. The adjustment comes slowly and painfully because what we are really forced to change is our inner selves.

I wanted to feel better. I was tired of hurting. I decided to start by working on my physical self. Recognizing that we were both becoming physically worn out from the stress, my husband and I started exercising together in the evenings. We resolved to begin using our dusty treadmill, and we also purchased a stationary exercise bike. It was difficult to motivate ourselves at the end of a long day when we really just wanted to lie down and vegetate, but exercising together helped. Darrell and I both noticed a difference in our energy levels after the first couple weeks of exercising.

We also decided to set aside an occasional evening as a "night off" from grieving, during which we would make a sincere effort to talk about something else. It didn't always work. Sometimes we just looked at travel magazines and dreamed aloud of vacations we knew we'd never take. One night we invited friends over to see if our concentration had returned enough to allow us to play cards.

I still had no enthusiasm for life. I was merely existing, stuck in a time warp. I longed to feel excited again about something, anything. The days dragged by. I wondered how many years I would continue to live, or simply exist, without our daughter. Indifference characterized my life.

Jeff was always busy. The one sure way I could get him to take the time to visit with me was to plan a road trip somewhere. In this way he would be alone in the car with me and have nothing better to do than talk to his mother. A conversation with Jeff during a two-hour ride to Grandma's house, over a year after Krista's death, provided the stimulus I needed to make some changes in my life.

---

"Mom, I think you forgot how to have fun."

"That's probably true, Jeff. What made you think about that?"

"You just don't seem very happy. You and Dad never go out with your friends anymore. I think you should. I feel happier when I do stuff with my friends. You should try it."

"I don't feel much like it, Jeff. When Krista died, part of me died, too. Maybe it was the part that liked having fun."

"She's not coming back, Mom."

"I know, Jeff."

"Mom, I think I'm getting used to not having Krista around. Sometimes I don't think about her."

Silence.

"How come I'm getting used to it?"

"It's okay not to think of her all the time. It's different for you, Jeff. It's not the same as being a parent. You'll have another family of your own someday. You and Krista were such a big part of my life. Sometimes I feel like I don't have a life anymore. I feel like half of it is gone. Do you understand what I mean?"

"Well, if part of your life is gone, then you need to get a new life. When I play sports, I'm so busy, I just think about sports, and I have a good time. You need to find something you like to do. You have to try, Mom."

I was touched by my son's concern. "You're right. I'll think about it. I'll try."

---

I thought about Jeff's advice a lot. I tried to think of something I used to enjoy that I might try doing again. Writing. I had enjoyed writing in high school. Maybe that would be a good outlet. I began writing this book as a result of my conversation with Jeff.

My new hobby as a writer opened up opportunities for growth as I attended workshops and met new people. I enjoyed the challenge of doing something different. Seeking other ways to grow, I went back to college to renew my teaching certificate and began taking computer courses. These diversionary activities made life interesting again.

Feeling revitalized, I became involved in volunteer work. My humanity was slowly returning. I began to care again, about my home, about my community, about other people. I discovered that the more time I spent involving myself with other people's needs, the less painful my loss became. As I reached out to other people, I became "connected" again with the present world, and experienced healing through this interaction.

Life is about circumstances and choices. Some decisions are made for us by circumstances. Of course, I did not choose to live without my daughter. Krista's death was beyond my control. How I will react to that death, and how that tragedy will affect the rest of my life, however, is my decision.

I can choose to dwell on the unfairness of life, focusing on my personal tragedy, retreating inward, oblivious to the lives of those around me. This choice will allow me to remain angry and withdrawn, becoming a bitter, self-centered person, crippled by emotional pain, incapable of love, and unable to find any joy in life ever again, because things didn't turn out exactly as I'd hoped or expected. People will avoid me. The love that exists in my heart will not grow; it will shrink. Death will have captured my soul.

There is another choice. I can acknowledge the great void in my life left by my child's death, and the fact that my old life died with my child. Realizing that none of us will live here forever, I can actively seek to build a different life. Love lives on. Love does not give up when life is tough.

There's a new song out by Mariah Carey called "Some Sweet Day." One line from it is "I never thought I'd have to live without your smile". That's exactly how I feel.

Much of our parenting was aimed at preparing our children to leave "the nest" and build a life of their own. We expected that someday Krista and Jeff would grow up, move out of the house, and start families of their own. Anticipating that we would not always be there to guide them, we attempted to prepare them by giving them a faith to live by, nurturing a positive self-concept, and instilling in them the virtues of hard work, determination and perseverance. We were preparing Krista to leave us to realize her own dreams; ironically, our dreams were shattered, and we became the ones who needed to build a new life.

During the early stages of my grief, I could do nothing more than endure the passing days. Survival required all my energy. But, the time came when I needed to make a decision regarding my own future. I made the decision I would have wanted my daughter to make. I chose life.

# THE GRAVE

As I travel Pleasant Ridge Road toward home, my van takes an unplanned right turn along a graveled path to yesterday. I hadn't intended to stop on my way home from town today, yet here I am again.

The bright green grass has been freshly mowed, and I can smell the sweet freshness left by the rainshower that ended only moments ago. Capable hands have meticulously trimmed around each headstone. Brightly colored artificial flowers decorate the hillside shouting of real love that hasn't died.

It is June. Krista has been dead eighteen months. Today I park the car and survey the spot where Krista's body lies. Some days it is enough just to check it out from the car and drive away, but today I need more.

I open the door and walk quickly through the wet grass, not even taking time to close the car door. As I slide my fingers over the surface of the headstone, the rose-colored granite feels hard and rough, such a contrast to our daughter's gentle spirit.

I trace the letters of her name:

*KRISTA LIN KIFER*

and remember the day her name was chosen.

Darrell and I were attending college. We had been dating for about a year, and we ate most of our meals together. I had an annoying habit of reading aloud anything lying on the table just because I liked the sound of the words.

I picked up a tiny white rectangular packet and read "'Crystalline sugar'...Darrell, wouldn't that be a great name for a girl--Crysta Lin? She'd be so sweet."

We both laughed.

"I like it," he said. "It's different. We'll name our first girl Crysta Lin."

So he wanted kids, too. Good.

When I became pregnant nine years later, I announced the good news with a NAME YOUR BABY book in hand. Darrell acted as though I were senile.

" We already have our names, don't we? Crysta Lin or Jeff Darrell?"

I shrugged my shoulders."We've had those names for so long. I thought maybe you'd be sick of them by now."

"No. I still like them."

It was decided. Because I was teaching elementary reading at the time, I felt the spelling had to be phonetically correct, so we changed it to Krista Lin. (I hated it when people gave kids names they couldn't spell until second grade. They don't have a choice with last names, so they really need a break on the others.)

Krista had smiled when we shared the story with her many years later; she had even related it to some of her classmates. It showed a weird side of her parents, but I think it made her feel special.

My lips move silently as I read the dates:

*January 17, 1979 - December 9, 1994*

Can she really be dead? I still can't believe it happened to us. She was only fifteen. I am reminded of our struggle to select the monument.

The phone calls started only two weeks after Krista's death. Each of the salesmen wanted to be the first to get his pitch in and sell us a monument. Their insensitivity infuriated me.

"My daughter just died," I whispered to the first caller. "I'm not ready."

After the fourth or fifth call, I was no longer nice. "My daughter just died. Leave me alone. If you call again, I won't even consider your company," I shouted as I slammed the receiver down.

I didn't want to pick out a monument for my daughter. I wanted to pick out a stereo or a new car, something fun that would make her smile. I wanted her to be alive, not dead. What was the big rush? They wanted to make the sale; they wanted money. It was just business to them. But it was the ultimate loss to us.

I had never thought much about graves and monuments before. Death seemed simple enough when people grew old. The body wears out and they die. No one lives forever. Death is the natural ending to a long life here on earth. The deceased would be deeply missed, but you knew their leaving you was inevitable. So you picked out a stone, listed the birth and death dates, added a name, and it was done. They had led a long, full life, and you celebrated their life even as you mourned their death. Most of them left children, grandchildren and great-grandchildren behind, a legacy for the future, reminders that their life mattered.

Selecting a monument wasn't that simple for Darrell and me. It was our daughter's monument, our last chance to do something for her physical body. Since we would be visiting that grave for many years to come, it was an important decision. Various salesmen pressured us to hurry and select one so it could be up for Memorial Day. A friend advised us to take our time because it didn't really matter when we did it; just wait until we were ready. I'm thankful for the advice of that special friend. It took a long time to decide what to put on the stone. We wanted something that would remind us of her life when we visited the site, not just her death. It's harder to select a monument for a child. When we selected our own headstones, we decided to list just our names, birthdates, and deathdates for the inscription. But, somehow, those bare facts didn't seem to be enough when a life was so short, so unfinished...

Darrell and I spent an afternoon walking through the graveyard locating other children's graves. Those monuments usually differed from adult grave markers by having something special engraved which gave a hint of the life the child enjoyed while he or she had lived. One infant's gravestone had a picture of a teddy bear. A fourteen-year-old's gravestone had a poem about fishing on it, along with an engraved picture of a trout stream. A seventeen-year-old who loved sports had his school letterjacket as part of a picture. These extras reminded me how much those children loved life.

Krista's class ring had come the day she died. She never saw it. We were going to give it to her for Christmas. My first instinct was to return the ring, but when I opened the box and saw what she had selected, I decided to keep it. She had chosen the school mascot on one side and the Christian symbol (Bible, cross, and candle) on the other. Sometimes I wear her class ring.

Our conversation about the ring was memorable. Krista had considered putting the Christian symbol on it. What did I think? I remember pointing out that most of the kids picked sports symbols or hobbies, and asking whether she'd wear it very much if it was different from everyone else's. We made it clear we didn't want to spend the money to have it sit in a box.

"I'll wear it, Mom. I'm not good at sports or anything. It's the only thing I can find in this book that says something about me."

We decided to use that symbol for the front of her monument, along with a heart inscribed, "*Child of God*."

As I stand before her grave,I focus on the single line across the bottom of the tombstone that says simply:

*WE MISS YOUR SMILE.*

That shy little smile was your trademark, Krista. Your first grade teacher wrote a notation on the sympathy card she sent: "What I remember most about Krista is her sweet, shy smile."

I especially remember the smiles you gave me when we shared a private joke. You knew me so well. We shared one of those smiles at Thanksgiving, our last holiday meal together, only a couple of weeks before you died.

As I took a bite of Aunt Jackie's homemade apple pie, I looked across the table into your x-ray eyes, wondering how I could hide the fact that this lovingly crafted homemade treat was not pleasing to my tastebuds. We both began to laugh hysterically--you because you knew I had to eat it--me, because you'd read my mind. I laughed so hard I was crying. When everyone else at the table looked at us suspiciously, I remarked, "Krista, stop making faces at me. I'm eating." They bought it, and we smiled triumphantly at each other because we'd pulled it off.

When we told Jeff about the words we'd chosen, he said, "She didn't smile all the time, you know. Sometimes she was a grouch."

"I know that, Jeff. But I still miss her smile."

Moments of silence.

"I miss having her to fight with. It really bugged you."

No response was required. I knew he meant it. Whenever I sent them upstairs to their bedrooms because I was tired of hearing them argue over some petty thing, I could hear the laughter as it trickled down the stairway into the kitchen. I knew their secret. It was all a plot to drive their parents crazy. They usually stayed in their own rooms about five minutes, then got together in Krista's room to read and listen to music. Mission accomplished.

I walk around to the back of the stone and read the epitaph.

*That which brings us sadness*
*has once brought us joy...*

This verse was taken from one of the sympathy cards we received. I keep my favorites in a special box in the upstairs reading room. They provide resource material when I feel alone and need to remember that someone cared. Grief can be so isolating.

There are some things I want to confess. Our relationship with our daughter was not perfect. Krista was a strong-willed child. We waited a long time for her and when she finally arrived, we spoiled her. Families are made up of imperfect humans. We made mistakes. We learned from them.

When Krista was twelve, she rebelled against our overprotectiveness by playing with matches one day when we were at work. That night our barn burned down when the smoldering ashes erupted in a giant blaze. We sought short-term family counseling to help Krista deal with the enormous guilt she felt. It was during these six weeks that I learned the importance of allowing children to take some reasonable risks. Perhaps it was also at this time Krista first became aware of the unconditional quality of parental love. Nothing she did would lessen our love for her.

Teenage years can be very rough. The year Krista turned thirteen was the most challenging to our mother-daughter relationship. She was determined to become more independent. I was stubbornly holding onto her too tightly because I wanted to keep my long-awaited child. We were engaged in a significantly disturbing power struggle for more than a year. We had the usual confrontations over dating, curfews, schoolwork, and especially the phone. She wanted more freedom. I was afraid to give it to her because I didn't want to lose her. I admitted I was overprotective. Was it really such a bad thing?

The turning point in our relationship was a conversation we had one evening in the upstairs hallway. She was in high school and felt that she should be allowed to ride in cars with other students.

"Don't you trust me? Why can't I ever go anyplace?"

"I trust you."

"Then, why?"

I spoke very slowly. "Krista, my greatest fear is that some night the police will appear at my door to tell me you died in a car accident." My voice was shaking. Had I been voicing every mother's greatest fear? Or was it a premonition?

She leaned against the doorway to her room. "Mom, if you never let me do anything because you're afraid I'll get hurt, I might as well be dead."

I was silent, thinking.

"I'm a teenager. I want to have some fun."

This scene replays in my mind often. Krista convinced me that I was suffocating her with my concern. She was almost fifteen years old when I finally summoned up the courage to begin to let go.

Understanding our worries, Krista was very conscientious about calling home if she was going to be late, or letting us know if her plans changed. Because she exhibited maturity and responsibility, Krista earned increased freedom rapidly. When I finally started treating her like the woman she was becoming, our relationship improved. We began to develop a deep friendship, the kind possible when mother and daughter accept each other as separate individuals, connected by love. I feel very fortunate to have this kind of relationship with my own mother. We confide in each other. We support each other. We go shopping and biking together. Although we live ninety miles apart, we usually manage to see each other at least once a month. Mom is one of my best friends. She would be my friend even if she wasn't my mother. I had hoped to maintain a similar friendship with my daughter.

I miss Krista's friendship. I miss going shopping together and eating lunch at Red Lobster. I miss the girl talk. I miss the notes.

Across the middle of the granite marker in cursive writing is a familiar trademark from the notes we left each other.

*We ♥ you, Krista.*

In small print across the bottom, the lines:

*Loving Daughter of Darrell and Carol*
*Caring Sister of Jeff*

We had asked Jeff to come up with a word to describe his sister, explaining that we were using the word loving. He was silent for about 30 seconds, thinking.

"She always took care of me and taught me things. How about 'caring sister'?"

Perfect.

Jeff does not go to Krista's grave. I wonder why he never wants to go there with us. "Are you afraid to go there?" I asked gently one day.

"No. I just don't feel the need."

Okay.

We do not insist that he go. His grief is not our grief. Sibling grief is real, too. I wish he had another sibling to share his grief. Darrell and I have each other in our parental grief.

I turn my attention to the grave beside Krista's. The name reads:

*JAMIE LYN BRAINARD*

Two white unicorns are etched on the rose-colored granite. How strange that both stones are the same color. It wasn't planned, but it seems fitting. The birthdate is September 11, 1978. The deathdate is the same as Krista's, December 9, 1994. Dead at sixteen.

When we moved to Monona, Krista was in seventh grade. Jamie, talkative and bubbly, was the first to befriend the new girl in town. It had been a case of opposites attracting. Their friendship survived the ups and downs of the usual petty teenage squabbles. When Krista's bookbag was returned to me a week after her death, I found a note in it from Jamie, dated the day they died, signed with their standard closing, "Lylas." It was an abbreviation for "Love you like a sis." They had been best friends. Now they lie side by side in two graves on the hillside.

Across the bottom of Jamie's headstone are the words:

*Daughter of Kevin and Janice*
*Sister of Kevin, Jr., and Kent*

---

Janice and I spent an afternoon together last December, anticipating our second Christmas without our girls. Although our daughters had been friends for several years, we parents had not developed any sort of real friendship prior to the accident. Now we attempted to share our sorrow during the more difficult times of the year. Janice and I went to a tree farm and selected a three-foot pine to put between the two graves for Christmas. We decorated the tree with tiny red bows. I added a brass dove with the words "Together in Christ." Jamie's mother hung a circular brass ornament decorated with two bears inscribed with the girls' names and red lettering that said "Best Friends." We cried together, and for that moment, I was connected to this woman as we shared our common grief.

Connecting was rare for me those days. For the first year after Krista's death, I was more of an observer than a participant in life.

---

I hear the distant whistle of the approaching monster train. It is time to leave the cemetery. The door of the van is still open. I jump in and hurriedly leave.

As I drive off, I stop halfway down the hill and glance over my left shoulder at the large planters of blue and gold flowers on Derek's grave. School colors. Derek should have graduated in May. I never met Derek Steva. He was seventeen, the driver, the oldest of the three teenagers who shared a death date.

Is it unhealthy to visit your child's grave often? Six months after Krista's death, a business associate asked me, "How often do you visit the grave?" Evidently, my answer was not satisfactory. His next comment was, "Do you think it's healthy to be visiting so often?"

My answer was, "If visiting the grave makes you feel better, it's healthy; if it makes you feel worse, maybe it's not. I need to go there."

He did not understand.

During those early months I needed to go to the grave often. Perhaps because a mother spends so much time tending to her child's physical needs from the moment of birth, it seemed almost natural to tend the place where her body now lies. Taking flowers to Krista's grave made me feel better because I felt as if I were still caring in a small way for her physical body which I longed to hold.

As time goes by, I find that I go there less often because I am adjusting to the loss of her physical presence, and I find increasing comfort in memories of special times together. Although Krista's body lies motionless in that grave, her spiritual essence remains forever in my heart and is with me wherever I am.

How do I decide when to visit the grave? Sometimes I go there on special days to take flowers or decorate a Christmas tree. More often, I do not plan to go there; I just end up there. I don't know why. It is as if my vehicle makes the decision at the last minute to turn into the cemetery instead of taking me safely home. I intend to pass by, but some days I cannot do so. I seem to be drawn there against my will. Is it because I need to cry even though I would prefer not to? Is Krista's spirit tugging at my heartstrings, begging me to shed the tears that bring temporary relief?

# WHEN WILL THE TEARS STOP?

What are tears? Webster's dictionary includes the following in its definition of tears: "a secretion of profuse tears that overflow the eyelids and dampen the face; an act of weeping; an act of grieving." Tears are a natural part of grief, as is crying. Examine the definition of crying: "to express grief, pain or distress by sobbing and weeping." By definition, tears are tools for grieving.

We are expected to cry and shed tears wildly when a loved one dies. Tears are an acceptable expression of grief during the mourning period, the days after the death and the funeral proceedings. Other people openly cry with us during this time of loss. But when the mourning period has ended in their minds, our tears remain. How do we deal with our tears then?

---

Eleven months have passed since Krista's accident. I am at work in a familiar office doing mundane tasks, keeping busy, pretending it is possible to live a normal life again. The woman from the real estate agency on the other end of the phone places a routine abstract order. I ask for her name and address so I can finish the paperwork.

"This is Krista," she answers matter-of-factly.

I am silent.

"Hello. Are you still there?"

*But my Krista is dead.* I take the pertinent information and retreat hastily to the bathroom because the tears are imminent.

Reminders, everywhere. I pick up the newspaper during coffee break and read of the death of a child in a fire. When the radio announcer reports a teenager's death, a car accident, a train accident, it is as though our tragedy is happening all over again, only the names are different. I cry because I know the extent of the pain those parents face, how drastically their lives will change. I cry because Krista is dead.

---

Tears can bring relief from pent-up emotions, but they can also cause embarrassment. Crying is still seen as a sign of weakness by many people in a society that values strength. It is ironic--tears can be medicine to heal the soul and at the same time a burden restricting the healing process.

The first six months I cried every time I attended church. It seemed so odd to be attending services without her. When I looked at the minister, I didn't see the flowing white robe behind the pulpit. I saw the man in the black derby hat standing at the door the night Krista died, bringing the bad news.

The hymns and the liturgy held totally new meanings for me. Everything made me cry. Sometimes I stayed home from church because I was afraid of the tears. When I discussed this with a Christian friend of mine, she told me when she assists up front on communion Sunday, many people are shedding quiet tears in church. God welcomes my tears, and I need His Word to dry them. So, I do what I must do. I go to church, and sometimes I leave early because the tears still come.

What makes me cry? I cry at baptisms and confirmations because they remind me of special days with my missing child. I cry when I see teenagers driving cars, working at jobs, having fun on dates, attaining goals, enjoying the kind of future Krista should have had. I cry at graduations and weddings because my daughter was unable to realize those dreams. The unfairness of life hurts. I cry on holidays, birthdays and special occasions because nothing is the same without Krista here.

The shortest verse in the Bible is "Jesus wept." Even Jesus, who had the power over death, was saddened by the death of his friend Lazarus. God understands my tears.

Even after our daughter has been dead for eighteen months, the tears still come at many inopportune times. But I can accept them now as a part of who I am. I regret the fact that my tears cause embarrassment to others or make them uncomfortable, but they are part of me.

During a weekend writing class I took at the college in Iowa City last May, I found myself drawn to the kindred spirit of a woman across the room. Why?

Lynn was a little younger than I, slender, pretty. Her posture was somewhat stiff, and I sensed she was uncomfortable being at the workshop. As we listened to various readings throughout the day, I glanced over at her and noticed tears forming in her eyes at the same moments that my own eyes were becoming excessively moist. It was obvious to me that this woman, too, was dealing with some type of deep loss. I did not approach her or attempt to invade her privacy to satisfy my curiosity.

One of our assignments in class was to rewrite Cinderella. My version was not a fairy tale, but a vision of my reality. I wrote from the viewpoint of the guardian angel who knew Cinderella was not going to live happily ever after for very long, and therefore made it possible for her to attend a special ball and have some beautiful experiences while she lived. As I read my version aloud, I cried, partly because I can no longer believe in fairy tales with happy endings, but mostly because Cinderella was my daughter's favorite story. The instructor was stunned by my reaction to this playful writing assignment.

When I left the classroom abruptly to deal privately with tears that could not be denied, Lynn followed me to the restroom to ask if there was anything she could do to help. I explained that the Cinderella story we were discussing had been my daughter's favorite story and that I was just feeling sad about her death. She added her tears to my own. Lynn understood my pain. Her mother had died several years before. Recently she had discovered she was physically unable to have children of her own. Lynn was mourning the death of all the parent-child relationships no longer possible for her. Our brief encounter lasted less than five minutes. We exchanged names and addresses and said we'd write; neither of us has. But I did write a poem that night as I thought of her.

For Lynn:

*When I looked at you across the room,*
*I sensed the grief of an empty womb;*
*Our pain is different, yet much the same,*
*A missing child bears the blame.*

*I cry for a daughter*
*I can no longer hold;*
*Your tears are for the dream*
*that did not unfold.*

I think of Lynn often. Some say you can't miss something you never had. It's not true. Perhaps an unrealized dream is the greatest loss of all. Who will comfort Lynn with words of sympathy? The loss of her dream is invisible to those around her, and she is left to deal with it alone. There are no memories to ease her pain.

Why is the loss of family so devastating? Family ties provide an undeniable connection between people. This connection provides one of our most basic human needs--a sense of belonging.

No one escapes emotional pain. Many suffer excruciating physical pain. Some hurts are just more obvious than others. As we reach out to each other in love, we become "connected" again and experience healing through our interaction. I do not believe that we are ever completely healed after losing a child. We are all searching for connections, to find our place in this world, to belong.

My great joy in response to Krista's life has been replaced by tears for the loss of her physical presence. Our capacity to love brings both joy and sorrow. The tears will not stop even when I die. They will be replaced by someone else's tears.

# MOTHER'S DAY

*It's Mother's Day and you're not here;*
*Forgive me when I shed a tear.*
*Days like this are extra tough;*
*I didn't get to hold you long enough.*

Today is Mother's Day. I miss you Krista. It's been a rough week for me. Everybody is making big plans to celebrate the day with their families. I still can't believe you're never coming home again. Everyone I see says "Happy Mother's Day." They mean well, but they don't understand how it really is this year.

I left a long-stemmed rose on your grave this morning. In a couple days it will wither and die, but it was wide open and beautiful today. It reminds me of you. You were here such a brief time, yet you blossomed from an infant into a beautiful young woman. A sensitive person, you were a fragile flower who brought joy to those who loved you while you were here. Now your body has withered and died. All we have is the memories of the special times we shared during your blooming time here on earth. It was far better to have held you for awhile than to never have known the joy of being your mother.

When someone gives me a rose, I appreciate its beauty until it withers. But even when it is finally discarded, I remember with love and fondness the one who gave me the rose. In the same way I remember you, Krista, and thank God for bringing you into my life. You were a rose in my life, and your death remains a thorn in my heart. I ♥ you always.

---

Krista was my firstborn. She gave me the gift of motherhood. I still remember the day she was born. As I looked into her innocent blue eyes, in awe of her perfect little features, I dreamed of the future we'd surely share. The emotional high I experienced when I held her little hand for the first time is a feeling I cannot explain, but if you are a mother, you know how great it was. We shared a host of "firsts" over the next fifteen years.

I recorded for posterity in her baby book her first words, her first foods, the first time she sat up, her first steps. She was the first to call me "Mom". Early photos preserve the memories of her first day of school, her first fishing trip, the first sled ride, the first bike ride, the first camping trip, and those special first holidays.

As she entered high school, we shared the excitement of her first Homecoming dance, her first prom, her Christian growth as she made her confirmation vows. I remember the anticipation of her first date, the heartbreak of her first breakup, the joy of her first love. She was becoming a young woman, and we were forced to let go and allow her to make many of her own decisions about the direction of her life. Sometimes we didn't agree with her choices. At other times we were surprised by her maturity.

I believe Krista knew how deeply we loved her. I remember telling her often that no matter what happened in her life, I would always love her; nothing would ever change that. Even her death has not lessened my love for her.

The last Mother's Day we spent together had been a beautiful, sunshiny Sunday. After enjoying brunch at a favorite restaurant, we had gone bike riding along the Mississippi River in Prairie du Chien, Wisconsin. We stopped for malts and sodas at a quaint little drugstore with a soda fountain. We were just the four of us, Krista and Jeff, Dad and I, having fun together. Krista's boyfriend had invited her to spend the day with him and his family, but she didn't go; she chose to spend the day with us. Family was always very important to Krista.

My final Mother's Day gift from Krista was a handwritten letter:

*Dear Mom,*

*You don't know exactly how much you mean. I don't know what I would ever do without you. You are there for me everytime I need you. Sure, I've had friends off and on, but you have been my friend through all the years.*

*You are always here to understand me. You are always here to laugh with me. You are always here to cry with me. You are always here to talk to me. You are always here to think with me. You are always here to love me.*

*I know that I am growing up and times are getting tough. But no matter how old I get, you'll always be my Mom. I love you Mom!*

*L♥ve,*
*Krista*

I am still her Mom. She is still my child. I love her always.

Our first Mother's Day without Krista was spent at home by ourselves. We had been invited to go out to eat with friends, and I know Jeff was disappointed when we didn't go. But I needed the freedom to cry, not the pressure of pretending everything was fine. I couldn't stand to go to a restaurant and see other people with their whole family, mothers and daughters together having a Happy Mother's Day. Not that first year. I needed to feel my sadness.

My friend Laura did not ask me if I had a Happy Mother's Day. When I saw her downtown a few days after the holiday, she merely commented, "Carol, Sunday must have been a really hard day for you. I was thinking about you." *Thank you, Laura, for understanding.* Laura, too, has experienced loss. She is not a stranger to grief.

I will soon be facing my second Mother's Day without Krista. This year will be different. I will still visit her grave and leave a rose in remembrance, perhaps pink because it was her favorite color, or red to symbolize the love we share. Tears from my eyes will water it abundantly as I remember the strawberry-haired girl I cannot hold. But this year I will also plan something special to do with my living child. Perhaps we will go bike riding or for a walk in the woods if the weather cooperates. Jeff also is a rose in my life, as are my husband, my parents, my sister and brother, and all those special people in my circle of love.

I see clearly now the necessity of creating memories today with all our loved ones, memories that will last a lifetime. There is no guarantee of tomorrow for any of us, regardless of age. Each of those special persons is an imperfect rose in bloom. I must give them all the love, all the smiles, all the hugs I can today, because roses don't last forever.

# DREAMS

Two kinds of dreams were affected by my daughter's untimely death. One kind represents a future shattered, the other, unconscious desires and distorted reality.

*Webster's Third New International Dictionary* gives the following definition: "dream of: to think of as possible, fitting, or proper." This describes the dream that began at Krista's birth, maybe even while she was still in the womb, of a future my child and I would share. It seemed possible, fitting, and proper that Krista would grow into an independent young woman, graduate from high school, attend college, establish a career, perhaps marry a man she loved, and give us grandchildren. Our parenting was aimed at helping those dreams become reality. But it didn't happen that way.

The same dictionary also gives these definitions for the noun: "dream: a series of thoughts, images, or emotions occurring during sleep: a semblance of reality or events occurring to one asleep: condensed, elaborated, symbolized, or otherwise distorted images of memories or of unconscious impulses experienced especially during sleep but also during other lapses in attention, the meaning of which is concealed from the ego." Many of the bereaved parents I talked with experienced this type of dream about their dead children.

In the beginning I was afraid to dream because I had only nightmares about the death, as discussed in my previous chapter on guilt. Several months after Krista's death, however, I began praying I would dream about her. I missed her so very much. I just wanted to be able to see her smile again and hear her voice. Other bereaved people told stories about how their departed loved ones contacted them. A father saw his dead son standing in a field on their farm. A husband talked with his deceased wife as she sat beside him on their bed. A dead mother smiled proudly at her daughter as she busied herself in the kitchen. Nothing similar happened to me. I felt so empty inside.

Some of Krista's school friends claimed they had seen Krista or heard her voice talking to them, that she was still spiritually present. I ached to feel her presence lingering, but all I felt was certainty that she had already passed on to her new life.

Six months after her death I experienced a dream about Krista. Like most dreams, it was all mixed up.

We were in a strange city, attending a church service in an unusual church. After the service, I had to climb an obstacle course to get out of the church, including rope ladders, swinging vines, and other goofy things. As I was about to go through the final tunnel leading out of the maze, Krista walked in.

"Hi Mommy. I came for a visit." She was a small child again with long, reddish blonde curls, wearing the brown jumper she had worn on her third birthday.

I threw my arms around her and held her tightly. She hugged me back enthusiastically. I was so happy to see her. I asked how long she could stay, and she said just for a few days, that she had to be back home for Christmas. Home? Holding her felt so good. I could finally ask her what I really needed to know.

"Is heaven better, do you like it better there?"

She didn't seem to comprehend my question. Maybe it wasn't possible to compare two such incomparable worlds.

"Better? It's different. I'm happy there." She smiled, but couldn't seem to find any words to explain it so I could understand.

I asked, "What's heaven like?"

Her face of innocence became a portrait of peace, with wisdom far beyond that of a child evident in her compassionate eyes. "There's lots of food...all the time, whatever you need, whatever you're hungry for..." Then she became a child again. "Where's Jeff? I want to play with him."

She jumped off my lap and ran to another room to join all the relatives. They recognized her right away and were glad to see her. Everyone knew instinctively that she was just visiting, but couldn't stay. Although Krista had been the oldest of her cousins when she died, in this dream she was younger than they were, and yet none of them questioned it. There was a ceremony of hugs. Krista came back to give me a really big hug, reminiscent of the good-night hugs we had always shared, before running off to play Hide-N-Seek. Now Jeff had a little sister to play with. It was so strange. When she talked it was obvious Krista remembered her own life here and knew what had been going on in our lives as well. In the dream she just wanted to spend some time playing with the other children she loved. I saw her go out the door during the Hide-N-Seek game and wondered if she could still be hurt if hit by a car out on the street. Feeling worried, I opened the door to follow her outside, and I woke up.

It made me so happy seeing Krista again and hearing her voice. I woke Darrell to tell him about my dream. A few minutes later, I became extremely sad, crying again, because I missed her so much. It was only a dream....

I tried to figure out why I dreamt of her as a little child instead of as a teenager. Darrell thought it was probably because I wished she were little again so I could know where she was and protect her from life's dangers.

I don't understand the meaning of my dream, but I am glad I had it. It seemed to confirm my belief that she was alright, bringing some measure of peace. I wish our loved ones could come back and visit us from time to time, but it would always be hard to let them go again.

Another dream occurred about a week after the first anniversary of her death. I began dreaming she were still alive. I had the same dream for several nights in a row. Because we had not been able to see the body, I could almost convince myself it might be true, that the report of her death had been just a mistake.

The dream began with her walking into the house, greeting me with a smile and a hug, as if she'd been gone for a night, then turning to go upstairs to her room.

I'd say, "Krista, you can't be here. You're dead."

Then she'd tell me the story of how she had escaped from the burning car through the back window and had been living someplace down south with motorists who had rescued her that night. She would describe sketchily the recovery process that eventually restored her memory and enabled her to come home to us. It wasn't hard to interpret this dream--wish fulfillment at its finest. This is the ending I wanted for my story of tragedy. This is the way the movie would end, or that wonderful escape mechanism, the novel. But it's not reality.

Our dreams are merely possibilities, some real, some imagined. Dreams acknowledge hope for the future. I need new dreams. Where can I find the courage to dream again?

# HOLIDAYS

Holidays are family times. Even the busiest of families pauses to enjoy a celebration complete with a festive meal and renewal of family ties.

I was probably one of the biggest holiday fans who ever lived. Christmas has been my favorite holiday ever since I was a child. It was Krista's favorite, too. We had to have a big tree, though none was ever quite big enough to suit me. I loved to decorate all the rooms in bright Christmas colors. Baking cookies and candies and wrapping gaily decorated packages were labors of love for me.

Now Christmas has become the most difficult time of the year for me because Krista is not here to share it. It is not just a special day without our daughter, but a whole season. The beauty of the first snowfall is dimmed by the knowledge it signals the start of a season of festivities Krista will not be able to participate in with us. Traditionally, our family decorated for Christmas the weekend following Thanksgiving. I liked to decorate early because the season always put us all in a festive mood. Now the decorations must wait until after December ninth, the anniversary of our daughter's death.

Our first Christmas without Krista came only weeks after her death. I was grateful for Christmas because the gift of Jesus was even more precious to us in our grief. We needed Christmas, but her death necessitated many changes in the Christmas celebration.

The gaily wrapped packages stacked on my closet shelf, lovingly selected for Krista, were given to a local charity. Only the gift selected for her by Jeff remained. He had picked out a special T-shirt she had asked for, and he didn't want anyone else to have it. Since it was a unisex shirt, we suggested he keep it for himself. Sometimes he wears it to sleep in.

It was our custom the night we decorated our tree to have a special dinner together, just our immediate family, after which each of the children received a new ornament to hang on the tree. But that first year it would have been too painful for the three of us to attempt the same custom. Instead, we invited three families of friends to help us decorate the tree.

I didn't feel inclined to bake, and many kind people supplied us with goodies. For the first time since our children were born, I didn't make a birthday cake for Jesus either, our traditional Christmas Eve dessert. We attended gatherings at our relatives' homes because we weren't up to entertaining. As we left on Christmas Eve, Jeff asked where the birthday cake was.

"Sorry, Jeff, I didn't make one this year."

Instead of attending Christmas Eve candlelight services at the Lutheran Church in my hometown, where I had celebrated it for almost forty years, we went with my brother's family to Christmas Mass at the Catholic Church. It was a beautiful service, and the priest's message touched on what Christmas meant for those of us whose loved ones were not with us to celebrate. We chose wisely that Christmas Eve. Jeff leaned over during the sermon and whispered, "He must know about Krista, Mom." It was a highly emotional Christmas for all of us.

Everything was different now and I couldn't pretend things were the same by keeping all the old traditions. Changing the holiday celebration helped us get through it the first year.

Krista had done her Christmas shopping the week-end before she died. She had a babysitting job during the summer and had done all her shopping with her own money for the first time. None of us knew what she had selected. We opened the packages she had wrapped for each of us.

Darrell received a Jenga game; Jeff got his Lion King Sega game; I received perfume and forest green bath towels.

Darrell hung the towels up for our guests after the holidays, and I angrily took them down again. I didn't want anyone else to use them. Selfish? Yes. Silly? Maybe. I feel close to Krista when I use them. I want them to last.

All of the first holidays were particularly difficult--New Year's Eve, Valentine's Day, Easter, Mother's Day, Memorial Day, Father's Day, 4th of July, Labor Day, Thanksgiving. The last holiday we spent together before Krista's death was Thanksgiving, and it was particularly traumatic to reach that holiday, acknowledging we had come full circle in a year of holidays without her. I found it very difficult to find something to be thankful for on that first lonely Thanksgiving.

Now we are working on this cycle of holidays a second time. It is not getting easier. But this Thanksgiving I found a reason to be thankful. One of these reasons is the way a mother and child are eternally connected.

Mothers and children are connected by an invisible cord. Unlike the cord that connects us until birth, this cord is not physical and can never be severed. It begins with awareness of our baby in the womb or the fulfillment of a dream come true when the child we have waited to adopt has finally arrived. The cord is made from a mother's love, binding us together forever, heart-to-heart. This cord is stronger than any earthly material. Nothing can destroy it.

When a mother and child are separated by death, the cord tugs at our heart, and we ache for the person at the other end of the cord. A mother's love never dies. When a mother can no longer hold her child's hand, the love remains. The cord is still there though no one can see it. It becomes our lifeline.

I am thankful we are connected this way. Mother and child--a bond death can't take away. Although Krista will not be with us physically at holidays for the rest of our lives, she will be a part of my celebration because she lives in my heart.

# WHERE ARE MY FRIENDS?

As I grieve, I am learning the true value of friendship. It is easy to be a friend when you share good times and laughter. Everyone wants to have fun. But we found not everyone is comfortable with our tears. Some of our friendships disappeared as we struggled with our grief.

Monica was a special friend. She was there for me daily for almost a year, caring for me in every possible way--cooking meals, calling on the phone, sending little gifts and cards. We were as close as sisters. Then, something changed. Monica stopped calling. I saw our friendship dying. When I asked what was wrong, she wouldn't discuss it. I'm not sure she knew.

I love Monica. I forgive her for abandoning me. Maybe she just got burned out. Maybe she thought it was time to be "over it." The changes I was making in my life bothered her. Perhaps she expected the old me to come back. Can't she understand that the old me died with Krista? I miss Monica, but I do not have energy to expend trying to recapture past moments of happiness. Our friendship was a casualty of my grief. I direct my momentum to the present.

I need a friend who will allow me to feel sad, who will help me smile again. My friend must learn to love the new me. She will not expect me to grieve perfectly because she accepts me as a human being with all my imperfections. She will forgive me when I am overcome by grief and do or say things unintentionally that require forgiveness. She will not abandon me in my time of need.

---

Laura was the friend I needed. She listened when I needed to talk. She did not run away or avoid me when stray tears streaked my face. Sometimes we cried together, or shared a healing hug. When I hibernated for weeks at a time, existing in a daily ritual of going to work and coming home to sleep, Laura sent cards or called to let me know she was still thinking of me, even though we seldom saw one another. She gave me space, yet made sure I was aware she was only a phone call away if I needed her.

When I called on a cold, winter afternoon, Laura came. She rescued me, helping me escape temporarily from the pain. We drove a hundred miles to Madison, Wisconsin and spent an entire day in the city. And for a few minutes that afternoon, as we roamed the shopping mall looking for bargains, I remembered what it was like to laugh with a friend. Our laughter made life bearable again.

Laura and I are still close. We enjoy occasional walks together and visit about our families, work and life in general. When I quit my job to pursue other interests as part of a search for meaning in my life, Laura supported my decisions. She understood my need for change. She rejoiced with me in my small victories--being able to eat at Red Lobster (Krista's favorite restaurant) without crying, learning to golf for the first time, having my first article published. A friend like Laura, an exquisite diamond, tough enough to endure life's trials without fading, is priceless.

---

A friend is anyone who affects my life in a positive way. I am adding a new class of friends that I designate "rubies." These are the people who come into my life for a specific purpose or to share a special gift that no one else can give. My encounter with these friends may be very brief, only a few minutes, several hours, or a memorable weekend. These rubies may not last as long as the diamonds, but they are equally as precious.

I discovered my first "ruby" two weeks after Krista's death. I finally summoned up the courage to venture out in public, deciding upon a morning trip to the grocery store so there wouldn't be so many people around. I had chosen wisely as the store was almost deserted that time of the day except for several older women doing their weekly shopping. Hazel, an elderly woman I recognized from church, was having difficulty getting a box off the top shelf. She was extremely short and somewhat bent over, apparently a natural result of the aging process. I asked if I could reach something for her. She smiled and thanked me politely, then asked my name. When I answered, there was instant recognition. She had read the story of our daughter's tragic accident in the local paper. There were tears in her eyes, and I knew we were both going to cry.

"I'm so sorry about your daughter," she said. But Hazel didn't stop there. Instead she gave me the special gift that was hers alone to give. "I know how it hurts. My daughter died, too, years ago. It still hurts."

Our tears were our bond. I felt God had sent me to the grocery store to meet this woman. She felt the same pain and lived with it. She was old. Had she lived with the pain a long time? I wasn't alone. Several days later I showed up at Hazel's house with a canister of homemade caramel corn. She was surprised that I had brought her a gift. She remains unaware of the special gift she gave me that day in the grocery store.

As part of my search to rebuild my life, I participated in writing workshops at several universities. Here, too, I encountered special people who enriched my life just by becoming a part of it for a short time.

Susan was immaculately dressed in a delicately flowered mid-calf skirt and beige knit top, her shoulder-length blonde hair perfectly framing her soft facial features. I avoided talking to her in the hotel lobby because I thought she was a model, and I felt awkward in her presence.

Learning she was taking the same writing class I was enrolled in, I summoned up the courage to introduce myself. I felt an undeniable connection to this woman the first time we conversed. She lived on the west coast and had flown to Iowa City for the weekend to immerse herself in writing, escaping the everyday hassles of city life. We spoke intimately about our pasts, joking about the possibility that we had been sisters in another life, or had walked parallel universes living the same life. My attendance at this workshop had been merely a diversionary activity, undertaken in hope of putting a little fun into my dreary life. The course was entitled "Writing for the Heck of It." Confessing my secret desire to become a published author did not bring snickers or raised eyebrows. Susan and I will probably never meet again, but she, too, had a positive effect on my life. That weekend at Iowa City I rediscovered a passion for writing.

I can make decisions that will lead me to people who can help me in my life's journey. New friendships can strengthen my desire to live again.

What about the casual friendships that got lost along the way--the Saturday night card club, the couples we once went dancing with? In all fairness, I must admit that invitations were extended to us. We just didn't have the energy or concentration to participate in recreational activities the first year after Krista died. We chose to let these friendships fade. When we were ready to participate in life again in this way, some of these relationships resurfaced with deliberate effort on our part, providing much needed diversion.

Some of our friendships were based on the fact that our children were of similar ages. Activities were planned together as families so the children had others to play with while the adults socialized. These friendships were very painful to maintain after Krista died. Watching their children continue to grow and participate in activities Krista might also have been enjoying created too much stress. Friendships based on this criterion alone did not thrive because we no longer had living children of similar ages.

I continue to actively search for friendship. Whereas family is limited, the possibilities for friendship are infinite. These friends are my treasures here on earth, added gratefully to the invisible ring of love that encircles my heart, holding it intact despite the broken pieces.

# THE MAIL STILL COMES

I open the mailbox and sort hastily through the stack of mail. It is another day of unpleasant surprises. There are two envelopes addressed to Krista today. One is from the American Institute of Commerce in Cedar Falls, Iowa, and one is from Concordia College. I should have just tossed them in the wastebasket. But instead, I open them and peruse the information. Both begin, "Dear High School Senior," and I am reminded again of the future my daughter cannot have.

Twenty months after Krista's death, she still gets mail several times a week--sweepstakes entries, record offers, technical school and college information, other junk mail. I wish the correspondence would stop. It upsets me. I have notified several of the schools and magazines that she is deceased by calling personally or writing to them. Her name must somehow be showing up on new mailing lists all the time.

I'm not the only person who finds the mail to be a problem. A friend of mine whose son died four years ago still gets junk mail addressed to him from time to time. Receiving no response, one of the colleges even called her house the summer after Steven should have graduated, four years after his death, and asked to speak to him. The eleven-year-old girl who answered the phone did not understand why someone was calling to talk to her dead brother. Handing her mother the phone, she did not speak, just went quietly to her room and closed the door.

How can I stop the mail? I don't know. I contacted the post office, but they can't just throw away mail when it is sent to a particular address. This is the computer age. There should be some central information number I could call to automatically notify everyone providing mailing lists that my daughter is dead. I have been unable to locate such a number. How do we get these names out of the system? If you have the answer, please let me know.

# INSURANCE

Money is a difficult subject to discuss among family members, harder still to discuss with strangers. It is obvious to everyone that financial hardship compounds a tragedy. But what about the effects of financial gain through a tragedy?

We had life insurance on Krista. It was not intended to provide the funds to bury her with. The $10,000 whole life cash value policy was intended to be her college fund. Our parents had set up similar funds for each of us when we were children, and we had cashed them in to pay for our educations. We also had purchased a $1,000 policy that guaranteed her insurability so that even if she developed a serious illness, she would be able to periodically add to her life insurance to provide adequately for her own family when she became an adult. Both of these policies were taken out to insure her success when she reached adulthood.

When the call came from the insurance agents wanting to make arrangements to pay off the claims, it felt like a giant slap in the face. I was rude to them over the phone. I knew her death wasn't their fault. I was just angry about being in this situation. We didn't want the money. We just wanted our daughter to be alive. The money was for her, not for us. Could we give up all our money and possessions and get Krista back? We would gladly make the trade, as would any parent. It was truly a sad day when we received the life insurance payments. Each check was another spike driven into my heart, further confirmation that Krista was really dead.

Do you understand car insurance? We were very ignorant about how it works. I assumed you carried the insurance to avoid hassles when someone was injured in your vehicle. If a policy stated $50,000 coverage per person, $100,000 per accident, to me that meant if someone was killed, their survivors would receive $50,000. After all, death is the ultimate injury, isn't it?

Since Krista was a passenger in someone else's vehicle at the time of the accident, we were automatically involved in an insurance claim whether we chose to be or not. A couple days after the funeral, an agent from the driver's insurance company called to schedule a visit with us. They were anxious to reach a settlement. We did not feel like discussing our daughter's death and told them so. But it soon became clear that we did not have the option of ignoring the insurance company.

A relative who was a lawyer explained that the insurance company had to pay out a wrongful death benefit when a death occurred, and we would not be left alone until it was settled. Informing him that Darrell and I did not want a lawsuit because we didn't want to cause additional pain to the driver's family, we asked this lawyer to settle for whatever insurance coverage the family had and be done with it. He knew it wasn't going to be that simple. Insurance companies are quick to accept premiums, but when it is time to pay a claim, they are slow, exhausting every possible angle to save money before paying any amount. They do this under the guise of being fair to their insured, but in truth, the premiums have already been paid and the money is coming out of the insurance company's pockets, not directly from the insured.

We were fortunate to find a competent lawyer to handle the negotiations for us. The insurance company needed evidence that Krista was a good kid and would be missed by her family. So we submitted photo albums, my journal, an autobiography written by Krista in eighth grade, and school records for their inspection. We found the process degrading, an uncomfortable intrusion on our privacy, to provide these materials. Krista had been an excellent student, maintaining honor roll status in high school, but what difference should that have made to the insurance company? Would we as her parents have loved her any less if she were a D student? Of course not.

I wondered why they needed those school records. How can one child's life be worth less than another's? Einstein was not a terrific student, neither was Benjamin Franklin or Abraham Lincoln. We don't know what our children might have contributed to the world.

A meeting was scheduled between representatives from the insurance company and our lawyer. Although our presence was requested, we decided not to attend. We were not up to the emotional trauma of discussing how much our daughter's life was worth. When the lawyer reported the results of the meeting to us, I was shocked. The insurance company had arrived at a settlement by using a complicated formula. They started with the amount of the insurance coverage, deducted the funeral costs paid by the railroad company, then deducted the amount that it would have cost us to send Krista to college for four years because she was a good student. I was outraged! How could they be so insensitive as to take into account money we supposedly saved by our child's death? Were we to have considered ourselves lucky not to spend all that money? If I had attended that meeting, the emotional outburst would have been ugly. And what if her grades had been bad? I imagine they would have arrived at a figure showing how much it would have cost us to continue to support her, assuming she probably wouldn't have gone to college nor made enough money to support herself. Were negotiations a game? Did the amount of the settlement determine a win or loss? They seemed to know all the angles. The price is wrong. No amount of money could possibly begin to compensate us for our loss.

Why do parents sue over the death of a child even though it cannot bring the child back? They do it because they want someone to acknowledge their loss and the fact that their child did not deserve to die. They sue over the unfairness of it all. Lawyers have traditionally taken a bad rap for instigating lawsuits. Our lawyer was the solution to our problem of dealing with the insensitivity of the insurance company. Do these corporate giants want us to believe our child's life was worth nothing? A child's life is priceless. Every parent knows that.

We shouldn't have to submit proof of our child's worth or be required to reveal the depth of our loss to strangers. This invasion of privacy only adds to the emotional strain we are already enduring.

Our lawyer reached an out-of-court settlement for us. We never had to discuss Krista's death with cold strangers. Yet the money has been a cross to bear because it feels like "blood money." It is not like winning the lottery. We have no reason to celebrate. How do we responsibly use funds that have come to us at such a tragic cost?

# MEMORIALS

I was under the impression that memorial gifts were donated to charities in memory of the deceased. I felt guilty using the money sent to us in cards for any of our costs, including the tombstone. My understanding of memorials has changed through my experience with loss.

First of all, if the death has caused a financial hardship, I believe the family should use money received from others to pay expenses, such as burial costs, or lost time from work. Grief is difficult enough without the stress of added financial worries.

A memorial can be a means of keeping the memory of someone we love alive. The ways in which we choose to remember our loved ones are personal and unique. Some people choose to give donations to parks, colleges, hospitals, or other institutions, which often list the person's name on a plaque so that he or she will be remembered for years to come. Others prefer private memorials given to help friends and family honor the beloved. We chose a combination of memorials.

We immediately set aside an amount to be used for scholarships to be presented to Krista's classmates during their senior year. The decision as to who would receive the funds was decided at a later date.

Every year on Krista's birthday, we select a special charity to give a present to in her memory, one that benefits children. There are so many needs that it's difficult to pick just one. The amount of the donation is unimportant; honoring our loved ones in this way is rewarding.

I think it's important to keep in mind that many scams do exist. Responsible giving means doing some research to be sure the money will be used wisely and for the intended purpose.

We did not lock in any long-term donations in Krista's memory, such as continuing scholarships, and I'm glad we made that choice. Our feelings change from year to year, and I like having the option of changing my mind and doing something different each year.

On the first Memorial Day after Krista died, we purchased a tree for each of the grandparents, aunts, and uncles to plant in their yards in her memory. Krista's young cousins refer to their mountain ash as their "Krista tree." We planted three evergreens in our own yard, in memory of the three teenagers who died together in the accident. When the trees grow larger, I plan to decorate them with Christmas lights, in remembrance of the teens' lights shining still in a far-off place. I have found these personal memorials especially meaningful, as did our extended family.

# FALL BLUES--BACK TO SCHOOL

September is here. After a dry summer the prematurely browning leaves signal an early fall. Changes reflecting Krista's absence are especially pronounced during this change of seasons. Again this year I took only one child school shopping in August when there should have been two. As I watch Jeff walk down our dead end road to board the bus this first day of school, I revisit the fantasyland of dreams unfulfilled.

Krista was a sophomore when she died. This would have been her senior year. No longer an underclassman, she would have enjoyed the advantages afforded seniors. She would have driven one of our cars to school, not ridden the bus, a senior perk. *Would she have been working at a fast-food restaurant, McDonald's or Hardee's, or maybe for our local telemarketing firm?* Why do I torture myself with dreams that can't come true? Why can't I just "get over it" as others think I should? Why can't I let go? Because motherhood doesn't vanish with the changing seasons, not even when one of the seasons is death.

I am thinking today of a five-year-old boy, a neighbor's son, who should have started first grade today. A tractor accident ended his life last June. I picture the sadness in his mother's eyes as the bus passes her house without stopping, the season of death having made it unnecessary to do so. Will she count the next twelve Septembers silently until he, too, would have been a senior?

Will next September be easier? Or will I start counting all over again with the college years? When will it end? Would it help if I could talk to someone who understands my lingering sadness?

*LEFT BEHIND*

Where can I find a friend for today, someone who can quietly listen, a hand to hold? I say a silent prayer today, for God to send a friend my way.

# PART III

# LIFE

*LEFT BEHIND*

*Life is a journey,*
*not a destination.*

*Expressways,*
*toll roads,*
*detours.*

*Take the trip--*
*relish the ride.*

# SEARCHING FOR JOY

Joy used to come more easily than it does these days. It was subtle, existing in the everyday happenings of family life. Now I find that I must search more deliberately for experiences that bring happiness to offset the undercurrent of sadness that permeates my life.

Where does one search for joy? Some seek it in material possessions or work or developing new hobbies and interests. Volunteer work can be extremely satisfying. I've known grieving parents who decided to have another child. They are not seeking to replace the child who died, as some may speculate. Bereaved parents know this is not possible. They are making a conscious attempt to experience joy again, and what greater joy is there than a new life to celebrate?

Joy and passion are closely related. To experience excitement about life, I believe you need to feel passionate about something you do. I have developed a passion for flowering plants. They are an ultimate expression of love to me. Flowers lend us their beauty for a short time, some of them blooming for only a single day, enriching our lives just by being there. I water them, weed them and fertilize them, seeking as my reward a few hours of breathtaking beauty. Do I ever feel it isn't worth my time because they don't last very long? No, I know they won't last. I am just searching for a moment's joy in their splendor.

I read the comics faithfully. I buy humorous books and attend movies that promise laughter. I try to find a reason to laugh at least once every day. Remember the age-old parlour game: "If you were marooned on a desert island for one year, what one thing would you take with you?" I need human interaction to survive. I'd take someone who could make me laugh. Life without laughter is like food without spice--not very interesting.

Taking time to appreciate the beauty of nature can bring a joyful sense of peace. Each season has its sensual treats--I enjoy them all: shuffling my feet through the crisp fallen leaves on a sunlit walk through the woods; awakening to the majestic sight of a crystal morning, trees and grass shimmering with winter frost; pondering the immenseness of creation as I witness the spectacle of a starlit night. Nature shouts of God's magnificence, and I am awed by what I can feel, see, smell, and hear at this moment. I forget temporarily my insignificant self.

Nature has always been particularly significant in Darrell's life.

---

One clear July evening when the stars were unusually bright, Darrell and I arrived home from a late movie, and I rushed into the house to say good night to Jeff. Darrell didn't come in. When I went outside to look for him, he was sitting on the front porch steps staring up at the sky.

"Are you okay?" I asked.

He smiled slightly. "Look how bright it is. The stars are so beautiful tonight. I wonder if they are celebrating something special in Heaven." We felt close to Krista just sitting there, quietly holding hands.

---

There are some definite advantages to country living. No streetlights interfere with nature's spectacular light shows. I find it impossible to gaze at the stars without thinking about the immensity of creation, confident that the life we know here is only a minute stopover on our journey.

Rainbows hold a similar fascination for me. I am not interested in them as a scientific phenomenon. I view them as the promise of a world beyond reality as we know it. Last May I was privileged to view the most magnificent rainbow I'd ever witnessed. I stopped my van on the side of the road where I could see both ends of it bending on the horizon and watched in awe. A flood of comforting warmth encompassed me as I sat reveling in its quiet beauty. Was Krista smiling at me through that rainbow? She had been fascinated by rainbows when she was alive and had even chosen to decorate her room with them. Sensing Krista's presence around me, mysteriously comforting and peaceful, I felt hugged.

Sometimes we can make a special effort to give ourselves five minutes of peace--a special kind of joy--by staging the scene. I remember a particularly difficult March day when the weather outside was cold, foggy, and drizzly. Let's face it --the weather does affect our moods.

I didn't feel like reading or watching TV or even having to be civil to anyone. I felt grouchy. I was restless. Exercising didn't help. I decided to pamper myself in an attempt to cheer myself up.

Selecting the perfect temperature, I drew a nice, hot bath, complete with bubbles. An easy-listening piano instrumental tape provided relaxing music. I strategically placed the dining room candles, usually reserved for special occasions, around the bathroom and lit them for no one else but me. I filled a wine glass with orange juice and topped it with half a pineapple slice. As I soaked in luxury, I began to relax, closing my eyes and imagining myself on a Caribbean beach, palm trees swaying in the breeze, a tropical drink in my hand, far away....

When Darrell came home from work that night, I was done being a grump. I may even have been smiling. He wondered about the candles in the bathroom. Bathing by candlelight seemed a little strange to him, especially in daylight. Yeah, it's strange. So what? Sometimes, strange is good.

My favorite place to find joy is in the arms of someone I love. Aren't hugs great? Do you have the urge to give a special someone unexpected joy right now by surprising him or her with a hug? Shared joy is doubly potent. I need a hug every day just to survive.

# YESTERDAY

Have you ever noticed how much enjoyment the elderly get from sharing stories about their younger days? It may be difficult for them to remember what happened yesterday, but they can still recall every detail of the night they picnicked with their children in the pasture, roasting hot dogs over the exploding hickory wood fire, or the day Johnny was stung by a swarm of bees, necessitating quick action by mother as she rolled him in mud to neutralize the spreading poison. We hear the same stories over and over and sometimes wonder why the narrator must dwell in the past. The smile on the character-worn face is reason enough to listen to the renditions again and again, rejoicing with the speaker in cherished memories.

I, too, have days when yesterday overtakes my present. Though I try hard to focus on the present, sometimes I need to retreat to the past in search of peace.

---

I find myself alone in the reading room upstairs. As I lift the photo album from the bottom shelf, I kneel on the floor, turning pages silently, recalling yesterday when Krista was alive.

Six months old--she is hugging Pooh Bear and chewing on his ear as she sits propped up with pillows on an overstuffed flowered couch. Two years old--Jennifer the calf is eating corn out of Krista's tiny hand. Daddy's helper looks like the perfect little farmhand in her red shirt and denim overalls. Four years old--dressed in red ruffles, Krista is having a party with her dolls and stuffed animals in the middle of the kitchen while I cook supper. Amidst child-sized rocking chairs, doll cradles, and high chairs, she pretends she is the mother nurturing all those she loves. Six years old--wearing braids and a blue and white jumper, our daughter is waiting eagerly for the bus to take her to her first full day of kindergarten.

School pictures. Kids change when they start school. They are never completely yours again. They think the teachers know more than you. Their friends know more than you. But your children still need you.

Birthday parties, holidays, vacations. I smile as I remember fond Kodak moments. Junior High--rapid changes. Krista's hairstyle changes often, part of her search for identity. She is dressed in blue jeans and a T-shirt. A touch of makeup accentuates her clear, blue eyes.

High School--adventures. Krista sits confidently astride a palomino on her first horse ride. Her face reflects her awe of nature as she sits on a snow-covered mountain above the clouds. On rare occasions, she enjoys dressing up--a black leather skirt and jacket for the homecoming dance; a shiny, teal, tea-length ruffled dress with rhinestone jewelry for prom. She looks so grown up; my little girl is becoming a woman.

The pictures stop. My smile fades. Krista will never be a woman. She died at fifteen. I cannot add pictures to the album, no new memories to fill the void in my heart. Instead, I pause to remember yesterday, because there I can find my daughter once again.

---

I know I cannot live in yesterday, but sometimes I need to go there for a while even though it hurts, just to visit. I don't want to forget her. Just as the man blinded by an accident cherishes the beauty of a world once seen knowing he will never actually see it again, I cherish memories of my daughter's life.

Happiness has a different meaning for me now. Only a couple weeks before Krista died, Darrell and I were driving home from a shopping trip to Dubuque. I remember telling him how happy I was, that I had everything I could ever want--two healthy children, a loving husband, a home, a good job. How lucky we felt! We had it all. I wish that I could feel that way again. No matter how good life is, Krista will always be missing. I will never have it all again. The happiness I hope for now is peace.

# CHANGES

I am a different person. My attitudes have changed. My priorities have changed. My goals have changed. Any traumatic event is life-changing for the people directly involved. The ways I have changed are personal and may not be the same for another grieving parent. I make no attempt to evaluate whether these changes are good or bad; they are simply the ways in which I have evolved during my personal grieving process.

Today is my birthday. It seems so strange that I am another year older and Krista no longer has birthdays. It is not the natural order of things.

Simple questions have become complex. How many children do you have? This question brought confused tears during the first year after Krista died. I did not know the answer. Only Jeff is here with me now, but I couldn't bring myself to deny Krista by answering "one." I still have two children. Jeff is thirteen and lives at home with us. Krista died at age 15 and lives in my heart. This is the only way I can answer the question and feel that I am being truthful. Perhaps in time the way I answer this question will change again.

I feel more responsible now for my own life. I once thought that God would protect me from life's dangers. I don't believe that anymore because He didn't protect Krista from the train. God's gift to me is life itself.

I think I am a little less demanding of my family. I used to act as though they were responsible for my happiness. Isn't it a terrible burden to make someone else feel responsible for your happiness? Loved ones can contribute greatly to your happiness, but they are not accountable for it. We all know people who seem to have everything, but are miserable. We all know genuinely happy people living under nightmarish circumstances. Although heavily influenced by environment, contentment and joy must be found within oneself.

I have always been a great worrier, not just about the big things, but about all the little things--failure, sickness, finances, appearances. Most of the things I worried about never happened. The one thing I worried most about did happen--my child died. All my worrying made no difference. It didn't prevent the disaster. It was wasted energy. I no longer treat everything as a matter of life and death. I have only one real worry now--losing another loved one to death.

Since Krista's death, Darrell and I have reevaluated the ways we spend our time. When a social occasion arises, we no longer ask, "Should we go?" but rather "How much do we want to go?" We each rate our desire to participate in potential activities on a scale of one to ten. If our total is above ten, we will probably both go; if it's below ten, we stay home. Zero means we definitely don't want to go; Ten means the outing is extremely important. If one of us rates the activity a ten and the other rates it zero, one of us may choose to go alone. I'm surprised at how many times we used to do something because we mistakenly believed it would make our partner happy when neither of us was really excited about doing it. We spend more time at home now, but we have a better time when we do go out because we really want to be there.

I have become more outspoken. I take risks in expressing an opinion on issues when someone else is likely to not agree with me. I don't always go with the flow. This has made me less popular in some circles, but that's okay. Do I care what someone else's opinion of me is? Not really. It used to hurt when I perceived someone disliked me or disapproved of something my family members did, but I don't care anymore. Compared to Krista's death, very few things have the power to hurt me deeply. Public opinion isn't one of them. Death still hurts, as does a friend's betrayal.

I had a conversation one afternoon with two other women about our teenage children's appearance. They were discussing how difficult it was to get the kids to dress up for church. Then, the conversation turned to the way some of the kids wear their hair and how we would react if a child came home with an earring in *his* ear or *her* nose. One mother remarked, "No child of mine would dare come home looking like that."

I couldn't shut my mouth, and my unsolicited opinion spilled out, "My child can come home with an earring if he wants. I wouldn't particularly like it, but it's just a fashion statement. He can also wear jeans and a T-shirt and tennis shoes to church. I'll just be happy to be sitting next to him in church. If he wants to shave his head, that's fine, too. It's his decision. I'll save the confrontations for the big things that really matter, like drinking, driving and drugs." The shocked look on the faces of the other women made it clear that my opinion was unappreciated. I doubted I would be included in any more of their conversations soon.

As I walked away, I wondered why I didn't keep my mouth shut. Where was my self-control? Where was my tact? I used to complain about the little things that Krista did or didn't do, too. When I hear people's petty complaints about their children now, it strikes a nerve deep within. I wish Krista was here to give me such problems.

Those of us who have lost a child to death seem less concerned with the superficial changes our surviving children make to express their individuality. Perhaps we remember squabbles over insignificant issues with our deceased child. We are more selective now in choosing issues that are worth fighting about. Our arguments are less about power struggles and public opinion and more about genuine concern for our children's best interests.

I follow my instincts more often. I remember how hard it was for us to decide to let Krista go to the prom as a freshman. Many of my friends let me know they wouldn't let their daughter go at that age. Children grow up too soon was the popular belief and the myth that followed was that if a teen went to prom as a freshman, she would have nothing to look forward to as a junior and senior. Krista was so excited about going; my instincts told me she needed that special night at the time. I'm glad we let her go.

Sometimes Krista did not like being a teenager. Older people would tell her just to enjoy it, that her high school days were the best days of her life. That comment made her angry. I assured her that the teenage years were indeed rough, the best was yet to come, and she would find life after high school to be the time when her dreams would be realized and life would be fun. Events proved me wrong. In Krista's case, the teenage years were the best years of her life.

I have become more selfish. My self-preservation instincts have been strengthened. I know what I can handle and avoid situations I am not ready for.

Graduations were difficult for me after Krista died. I have already decided not to attend graduations this year since it is the year Krista should have graduated from high school. It would be too difficult to watch her classmates graduate without her. Why should I torture myself? We will send cards this year, sparing those that invite us the embarassment of dealing with our tears as they celebrate this joyous occasion.

On the first anniversary of Krista's death, I took a vacation day and stayed home where I could cry in peace. I also took a vacation day from work on the first two missed birthdays. There are days when it is impossible to pretend things are fine. But on the second anniversary of Krista's death I taught school. Afterwards, I stopped at the greenhouse for flowers, and visited the cemetery to grieve privately. I also taught school on her third missed birthday. She would have been eighteen. One of the kids in my fourth grade class celebrated his birthday that day, and it was a struggle to restrain the tears. But I made it through the day, working and keeping busy. As I laid a rose on Krista's grave that afternoon, I realized some healing had taken place the previous two years. I had progressed from the stage of uncontrollable grief to the level of coping with the reality of the situation.

In many ways the second year without Krista was more difficult than the first. Whereas during the first year I was dependent upon those physically near me to keep me busy and give support, much of this support disappeared after the first year. People mistakenly believed, I suppose, that my surviving the first year meant the worst was over. In reality, as the time since I last hugged Krista lengthened, the loneliness became less bearable. I turned then to my extended family, despite the many miles separating us.

Other than Darrell and Jeff, my sister, Sher, and my mother were my strongest support system during the second year. Blood ties are different than those of friendship. Because they shared a past of family ties with Krista, Mom and Sher could talk to me about her, helping keep her memory alive. When the initial shock of loss wears off, those memories are a necessary lifeline for the grieving survivors. Although friends understood that I had lost someone very special to me, they had not had a close relationship with Krista and could forget her. My friends did not miss her. I needed someone who would mention Krista's name, who could remember with me my beautiful, sensitive daughter. If no one remembers your loved one with you, it is almost as though the person is being killed a second time. Whereas my mother and I have always been close, I feel closer to my sister now than ever before.

My long distance phone charges during the second year were horrendous. When Sher and I each married and went off to start our own very different lives, our relationship became less intense, more superficial. After Krista's death, Sher and I became intimately reacquainted through our long phone conversations. As we shared our disappointments with life, our feelings and attitudes, our hopes for the future, we discovered that we are not as different as we once imagined. We have re-established our bonds of sisterhood. I love Sher. I have always admired and respected her. Now I realize how much I need her. Sometimes, when I call her, neither of us has anything important to say. Yet, there is comfort in the silence, just knowing she is there at the other end of the phone. Friends come and go as today's mobile society moves around the country, but family relationships properly nurtured endure. I am grateful for Sher's continuing presence in my life.

I no longer assume that I or any of my loved ones has a lengthy future. I hope we do. But I do not count on it. I prefer to make decisions based on what feels right for today. That may mean I'll spend money taking a trip to build new memories rather than building a retirement fund. It means I'll spend more time playing with my loved ones, young and old alike, and less time cleaning house. I'll grab the gusto of today instead of waiting for tomorrow's promise to fulfill me.

I have no time for grudges. I can't wait to settle differences, apologize, forgive or be forgiven. One of us might not be here tomorrow. It may be too late. Now is the time to straighten things out.

This could be my last day on earth. That thought does not frighten me. Realizing my time here is limited makes my time valuable. I want to spend it doing things I feel are worthwhile. Let me acknowledge here that what does not seem worthwhile to me may be crucially important to someone else. Staying in touch with my own values makes it easier to say "No" when I am asked to do something I consider irrelevant. It also makes it easier to say "yes" when I have an opportunity to do something I really want to do, no matter how busy I seem to be.

My house is sometimes messy and would certainly never pass the white glove test. I seldom choose caring for my house over caring for people. I clean house when I have time. The dust will always be there. That isn't true of the people in my life.

I have lots of time for people. Time spent listening, talking, laughing or crying with friends, loved ones, or strangers, is never wasted time.

# TODAY

Moments ago I threw popcorn to the ducks as I walked along the river enjoying the bright midday sun. As I sit on the weather-worn park bench, the warmth of the sun's rays upon my skin is tantalizing, comforting, mysterious. If I close my eyes tightly, I cannot see the sun, yet I know it is there because I can feel its presence so strongly. In the dark of night when I can neither see nor feel it, it still exists.

God's presence in my life is like the sun: sometimes I feel it strongly, sometimes I cannot feel it at all, but always it is there. Even when I'm feeling lonely and vulnerable, I am not really alone.

Hope for tomorrow is not enough. I am not biding my time, waiting for death to reunite me with my loved ones. I have things to do before tomorrow comes. I have love to give, lessons to learn, people I've yet to meet. I am curious about you, the stranger I've not yet met. I want to discover the connection that will make us friends.

What will I do today? The possibilities are endless. I decide where I will go, what I want to accomplish, my goals for this brand new twenty-four hours. I may run into some unexpected detours along the way, but I won't be afraid of what is around the corner. I will remember that life is an adventure.

I often begin my day by writing. Why do I write? I write because paper is my friend. It accepts all that I tell it nonjudgmentally. It listens to my thoughts with no interruptions. I can be the real me, expressing my opinions and emotions freely without worrying about its reaction. It does not betray my confidences, but allows me, alone, to decide which of my reflections are to be shared with others.

Paper cannot laugh at my mistakes, my fears, my dreams, my illusions. It is only paper.

My journal records my changing moods--happy, sad, angry, confused, or amused. Sometimes I write to remember; other times, I write to forget. Writing helps me get thoughts out of my head so I can be at peace, or into my head so I can solve a problem. I write because I want to laugh or need to cry.

My goal for today is simple. I want to make one person smile. If I can accomplish that, I will feel that my life had meaning today.

I have arrived at a deeper appreciation of people, not just close friends and family, but also the strangers I encounter as I go about the daily business of living. I am grateful for the friendly postal worker who greets me with a smile each time I go to the window to buy stamps. I really need that smile. Today I thanked her for doing her job well, and for brightening my day with her cheerful attitude.

I feel the same appreciation for the store clerk and the secretary. How often do they have to deal with impatient, complaining customers? People tend to be very vocal about poor service. I think we should be just as quick to give honest compliments for a job well done. Not only will we build the recipient's self-esteem, but expressing gratitude builds our own character. As we appreciate others around us, we become more positive about life.

Writing is a solitary endeavor. I must make a conscious effort to get out of the house every now and then and expose myself to the possibility of meeting new people. Incidents over the last couple of years have convinced me that people are all connected in some way. If only we had the time to visit with the strangers we encounter, I think we'd be amazed at the high incidence of connecting threads that run through our lives.

---

Darrell came home from work one day about twenty-two months after Krista died and recited a strange turn of the day's events. He had recently rented a hog building about four miles from our home and hired a man that was recommended by another farmer to power wash the building to disinfect it for our use. Since the man resided in a town seventy miles from Monona, Darrell arranged to meet him in town to give him a ride to the country location. Following complicated directions to find the right farm would have been difficult. As they rode together, the two men were remarking casually on the beauty of the fall season and the spectacle of the colored leaves that abounded on the hillsides along the Mississippi River. The stranger commented that in spite of the beauty, the hills in this area posed problems. His nineteen-year-old daughter had died in a car accident in this area five years before. Darrell gently questioned the man for further details. Because of the hills, the man said, the teenager had been unable to see an approaching train at an unmarked railroad crossing near Postville. Investigation of the accident site showed that she had stopped, but as she'd started across the tracks, she had been hit full speed by the train engine as it emerged suddenly from behind a small grove of trees. The young woman died instantly. Darrell amazed the grieving father by confessing that our daughter had been killed at the same crossing. The two men sat in a pickup truck on the side of the road and talked, no longer strangers at all, but two fathers having an intimate conversation about the loss of their beloved daughters. A connection was made.

This man was involved in a lawsuit for several years after his daughter's accident in which he attempted unsuccessfully to get the Department of Transportation to install lights and crossing signals. Would our daughter's fate have been different if his lawsuit had succeeded?

---

Sometimes fate brings people together in unexpected ways. It amazes me that these two men not only met but also ended up in such an intimate conversation. Most of the men I know don't easily discuss personal issues with friends, and would be less likely to have such a discussion with strangers.

Even when we concentrate on living in the present, the past is always part of us, surfacing at unexpected times, reminding us of who we are. We cannot escape its grip.

Recently Darrell and I attended a special Girl Scout award ceremony honoring local teenaged girls who had earned the Gold Award, the highest achievement in scouting. After receiving their awards, each of the six recipients presented her parents with a rose and an affectionate hug, thanking them for assisting her in reaching her goal. I hadn't expected the day to be difficult, but as I watched the exchange of hugs, I couldn't stop the tears that dampened my face. I wanted so much to be able to share a hug like that with Krista again. When we arrived home, I asked Darrell what he thought of the ceremony. He said it was really difficult for him when the girls were hugging their parents. He wanted a hug from his daughter, too. So it wasn't just me. Her absence still hurts. I want to laugh again. And I do laugh, often. But I can never forget that I have cried.

Almost two years after Krista's death, I attended a funeral for the first time since her burial. The service was for an eleven-day-old boy. Dressed in royal blue velour overalls with a soft white shirt, the blonde-haired Michael looked as perfect as a delicately fashioned porcelain doll. He lay motionless on a white satin cushion in the miniature coffin. Was he really dead? Why did I have the overwhelming urge to pick him up and hug him? I felt such empathy for the parents and grandparents. I cried during the funeral. I had fifteen years of memories to comfort me. They had only eleven days. They didn't even get to spend one holiday together.

The minister had a difficult time getting through the service. His voice shook, and I suspected he was close to tears. It made me wonder about ministers. Some of the funeral services I've been to are so personal and moving, while others are cold and impersonal. Do some ministers seek to keep the service impersonal because they are afraid they will not be able to get through it without an emotional breakdown? Are ministers uncomfortable with death, too? Do they see the betrayal of their emotions as a lack of faith? I found the trace of emotion released during the service made it more real. How can any human being be untouched by the death of a child?

Grandma was a very wise woman. I remember her telling me once that when life gets you down and you begin to feel sorry for yourself, you need to find somebody who is hurting and do something about it. She didn't have any fancy degrees in psychology, but Grandma understood the human heart. Helping feels good.

Who is hurting? Everyone has problems. Some deal with difficult issues like death, divorce, or illness. Others suffer loneliness, boredom, lack of leisure time. The elderly are often forgotten and appreciate home visits. A busy friend would be delighted to receive a home-cooked meal or dessert when she comes home from work. Helping is showing you care.

It works for me. I got a thank you note for delivering flowers from my garden to a sick friend. But this seemed backwards. My joy in being able to share the flowers was probably greater than hers in receiving them. By accepting my gift happily, she had made my day.

I have quit my job as a secretary. It was difficult concentrating on paperwork after Krista died. I needed to work with people.

Currently I am working as a substitute teacher. The call comes early in the morning in response to the illness or another emergency of a teacher. It will be an exciting day. I seldom know the children I will be teaching. The day will be full of surprises, and the only assurance I have is that I will not be bored. Usually, the kids are great, and I remember why I love teaching. Children aren't round pegs that fit in neat little round holes. Each child is unique, and the younger they are, the less they have been trained to give up that special uniqueness in favor of conformity.

I tried substitute teaching when my children were small and found it difficult to go into a classroom not knowing what to expect. I needed more control over my day. I wanted to do a good job and felt inadequate when I didn't get everything accomplished that the teacher had planned. I was a perfectionist.

My new personality is more suited to this job. One can't be a perfectionist and be happy substitute teaching because things just don't go as smoothly as they do for the regular teacher. I realize I am there only for a day and so I do the best I can. That has to be good enough. It can be very trying some days. If I can keep a sense of humor, not only with the children, but also toward myself, I can manage. The eight hours at school seem to pass very quickly. If the class is really difficult, I don't have to go back again. I have that option. I can handle anything for just one day. Teaching occupies my mind and my body. It is fun. And I get that necessary bonus, a paycheck.

This doesn't mean I'll be teaching until I retire. I'm still changing. Maybe tomorrow I'll pursue another interest. Change no longer frightens me.

I arrive home before Jeff. He is either at basketball or track practice. I try not to substitute on game days.

Watching him play sports is a priority. Jeff is always starved after practice, so we usually share a snack when he gets home and visit about the day's activities. Jeff spends a lot of his time talking on the telephone. That's how teenagers are. I am grateful for a few minutes of uninterrupted conversation with him.

The three of us gather around the kitchen table for our evening meal. I no longer set four places by mistake. We have adjusted. There is a new kind of "normal" at our house. Jeff shares tales of life in Junior High, changing the names, of course, to protect the guilty (mothers do talk, you know). We usually get a healthy dose of laughter this time of day. Sometimes Darrell shares the new jokes he has heard from customers or salesmen, if he can remember the punchline. Jeff is amused by my story of a hard day in kindergarten--story time, coloring skills, nap time, recess, milk and cookie break, and the most difficult one of all, free play.

Jeff will be in high school next year. We're considering hosting a foreign exchange student. The thought of sharing our home with someone from another culture is exciting. We could use a little excitement around here.

When Jeff goes off to college in four years, we will adjust again. Will the adjustment be easier the next time? I think so. I will hope that he is coming home again, and if I miss him, he will be only a phone call away. I will rejoice when he has a chance to make his dreams come true.

Life is good. It's not everything I hoped or planned, but it still has its moments. I am at peace with myself, with God, with reality.

## APPENDIX

**WHERE TO FIND SUPPORT GROUPS:**

To locate formal support groups available in your area, contact area hospitals, churches and hospices. These organizations often sponsor grief support meetings, or have knowledge of those available.

Contact these national organizations designed specifically to help parents in grief to get on the mailing list of the regional support group nearest you.

The Compassionate Friends
P.O. Box 3696
Oak Brook, IL 60522
(630) 990-0010

The American Sudden Infant
Death Syndrome Institute
6065 Roswell Road, Suite 876
Atlanta, GA 30328
(800) 232-SIDS
In Georgia, (800) 847-SIDS

**SUGGESTED READING LIST:**

**General Grief:**

Wiersbe, David W.. *Gone But Not Lost (Grieving the Death of a Child)*. Baker Book House, Grand Rapids, Michigan (1992). (a good book to read first)

*Bereavement: A Magazine of Hope and Healing*. Bereavement Publishing, Inc., 8133 Telegraph Drive, Colorado Springs, Colorado 80920-7169.
(grief magazine published bi-monthly; stories and poems submitted by the bereaved)

Richards, M. Gregory. *When Someone You Know is Hurting*. Zondervan Publishing House, Grand Rapids, Michigan (1994).

Manning, Doug. *Don't Take My Grief Away From Me*. In-Sight Books, Inc., P.O. Box 2058, Hereford, TX (1979).

Taylor, Patrick. *When Life is Changed Forever: By the Death of Someone Near*. Harvest House Publishers, Eugene, Oregon (1992).

**Personal Experience**:

Davies, Ray. *A Song for Marty*. Rudi Publishing, 1902 Broadway, Suite 3221, Iowa City, IA (1992).
(loss of a son--car accident)

Chilstrom, Corinne. *Andrew, You Died Too Soon*. Augsburg Fortress, Minneapolis, MN (1993).
(loss of a son--suicide)

Beattie, Melody. *The Lessons of Love*. HarperCollins Publishers, New York, NY (1994).
(loss of a son--skiing accident)

Johnson, Barbara. *Stick a Geranium in Your Hat and Be Happy*. Word Publishing (1990).
(finding humor in the midst of pain)

**Men's Grief**:

Golden, Thomas R., LCSW. *Swallowed By a Snake: The Gift of the Masculine Side of Healing*. Golden Healing Publishing LLC., Kensington, Maryland (1996).

Staudacher, Carol. *Men and Grief*. New Harbinger Publications, Inc., Oakland, CA. (1991).

**Spiritual/Inspiration**:

Ban Breathnach, Sarah. *SIMPLE ABUNDANCE, A Daybook of Comfort and Joy*. Warner Books, Inc., 1271 Avenue of the Americas, New York, NY 10020 (1995). (enjoying life)

Staudacher, Carol. *A TIME TO GRIEVE, Meditations for Healing After the Death of a Loved One*. Harper San Francisco, A Division of Harper Collins Publishers (1994).

Eadie, Betty J. *Embraced by the Light*. A Bantam Book. (Bantam edition Oct. 1994). (Gold Leaf Press edition 1992). Gold Leaf Press, 537 Main Street, Placerville, CA. (near-death experiences)

# *LEFT BEHIND*

*A Mother's Grief*

ISBN 0-9666014-0-8

## Order Form

To order additional copies, please complete this form and send it to Paz Publications, P.O. Box 16, St. Olaf, IA 52072.

(If you are ordering this book as a gift for a bereaved parent and would like the author to personalize the book, please include the name of the parent, name and age of the deceased child, and cause of death. Send the order form to Carol Kifer, c/o Paz Publications at the above address.)

Name ____________________

Address ____________________

City ____________ State ________ Zip ____________

Number of copies ______ (@ $12.95 each) $ ________

Sales Tax 6% (Iowa residents only) ________

Shipping & Handling ($2.50 first copy; $.50 each additional copy) $ ________

Total Cost $ ________

Please do not send cash. All checks should be made to *PAZ PUBLICATIONS*. All orders must be prepaid. No C.O.D. orders.

(319) 539-2055

## *ENDINGS*

*When you were small, we read fairy tales*
*that ended "happily ever after";*
*But real life endings*
*can mean living with disaster.*

*Your death brought us grief,*
*sorrow, and unending pain--*
*Nothing in this life*
*will ever be the same again.*

*We thought we had time*
*to laugh and to play;*
*Now we know--*
*all anyone has is TODAY.*

*My Child, we know*
*that you are all right;*
*We pray for the courage*
*to get up and fight.*

*OUR LOVE FOR YOU LIVES ON,*
*FOREVER, you see;*
*Finding ways to express it--*
*that is the key.*